THE ART OF THE INTERVIEW

THE ART OF THE
INTERVIEW

A GUIDE TO INSIGHTFUL INTERVIEWING

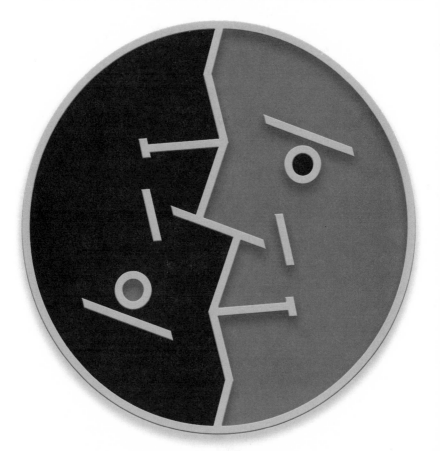

MARTIN PERLICH

SILMAN-JAMES PRESS   LOS ANGELES

Copyright © 2007 by Martin Perlich

10 9 8 7 6 5 4 3 2 1

Library of Congress Cataloging-in-Publication Data

Perlich, Martin.
The art of the interview : a guide to insightful interviewing / Martin Perlich.
    p. cm.
Includes index.
ISBN 978-1-879505-93-3 (alk. paper)
1. Interviewing in journalism. I. Title.

PN4784.I6P49 2007
070.4'3--dc22
2007004606

Cover design by Wade Lageose

Printed and bound in the United States of America

Silman-James Press
1181 Angelo Drive
Beverly Hills, CA 90210

Quot Homines Tot Sententiae.
(So many men, so many questions.)

—Terence (185 B.C.–159 B.C.)

Contents

Foreword

The interview art form is an excellent example of contingent design. There is the problem of how to handle your guests and their interests, there is the opportunity to add value to your own life and enrich the lives of others, and there are those unexpected contingencies. If it were not for the contingent, the preparation for an interview might be like writing an algorithm, a directive for proceeding along a well-defined path. Yet the best interviews explore, entering new territories, drawing novel perspectives. The same could be said of Martin Perlich's *The Art of the Interview*, which has a Zen-like quality reminiscent of *The Art of Motorcycle Maintenance* some may remember.

Ezra Pound speaks of the best planner as being the one of whom the people can say, *We did it ourselves*. I recall talking to the composer Vaughan Williams about his music for the film *Scott of the Antarctic*. He characteristically remarked that he wished I had not mentioned it, for the best film music accompanies the moods and events in ways that should not be noticed for itself. Surely, the art of the interview is like that. The interviewer is remembered for the performance of the people being interviewed: those interviewed may say, *We did it ourselves*.

Martin Perlich's leading message is twofold: prepare, listen. How often are we subjected today to the celebrity interviewer who seems to know everything under the sun and jabbers on while his truly celebrated subject sits by, barely given time for a sound bite? Too often. Let us not forget the strongly gentle interviewer, who brings forward rare and treasured moments. This book offers that precious opportunity.

Whether you just enjoy hearing an interview or you love intelligent conversation, or you aspire to some professional role as an interviewer, or are a professional already, or you are someone who has been or might be interviewed, this book has something for you.

—Lionel March
Former Rector of the Royal College of Art, London

Preface

I have arranged *The Art of the Interview* in a systematic, easy-to-use format that allows anyone, from a first-time user to a seasoned professional, to find and take from it whatever he or she needs: from basic structures and practical procedures to advanced "inside-the-head" concepts and methods.

For 40 years, in virtually all media, I have conducted practically every type of interview—celebrity, political, author, sports, arts, scientific—in all types of formats—print, radio, TV, film, Internet, recorded, and live broadcast. I've worked with a broad spectrum of public figures, celebrities and politicians, and regular people who happen to find themselves in front of my microphone. I was never schooled in broadcast. What I present here is culled from what I've experienced, and I've drawn certain conclusions regarding general rules, guidelines, and stratagems that I believe will be helpful to you. I have included a number of interview anecdotes, which will serve to illuminate the text. Take from the book whatever you need, but, above all, *enjoy it*—and the interviews it will certainly facilitate.

Pace e Luce
MP

*Nature has given man one tongue and two ears,
that we may hear twice as much
as we may speak.*
—Epictetus (55 A.D.–135 A.D.)

1

The Two Rules of the Interview

Even if you have the chance to read only the first page of this book, you can learn the foundation for everything you need to know about the art of interviewing. There are only two rules:

1. Prepare
2. Listen

From these two principles the whole craft of interviewing flows, from the simplest sound bite to the most complex character portrait. I'll give you an example from my own life—my introduction to interviewing.

A long time ago in a Cleveland far, far away, I was working the cash register at Discount Records on Public Square. The phone rang. Expecting yet another request for Mantovani or Alan Sherman or Ray Coniff, I was pleasantly surprised to hear the mellow pipes of a certain Bob Conrad, Program Director of the local classical radio station, WCLV.

For the last year I'd been doing a weekly show on 'CLV called *The Audition Booth*, where I reviewed new releases. The program was sponsored by the very retail record chain where I was a puny assistant manager. I was unpaid for my broadcasting efforts (and earning every penny), but our classical record sales had increased significantly as a direct result of the show, so I at least got the satisfaction of knowing I was doing a pretty good job. Conrad's call was nonetheless unusual. As was his custom, he came right to the point.

"We want you to interview Leonard Bernstein."

"Me? Why me?"

"Everyone on my staff is afraid."

"Afraid of what?" I had the phone between my ear and my shoulder, so I could keep bagging records.

"We all think you're the best person to do it."

"Come on, Bob. I'm not even a professional. (Thank you, sir. Enjoy your purchase.) I've never done an interview in my life," I temporized truthfully.

"It doesn't matter, Martin," he countered, a little *too* patiently. "I'll be your engineer. You just talk to the Maestro."

"About what? Records?"

"It's the first local New York Philharmonic appearance since 1920 or something."

Actually, Leonard Bernstein's appearance in Cleveland was the media event of the season. He would be conducting the same great orchestra he led on his famous *Young People's Concerts* series on CBS television.

"So I hype the concert?"

"Martin, he's Leonard Bernstein! Anything he says will hype the concert!"

Luckily (and atypically for me in those days) I had the sense to shut my mouth and accept the opportunity he was offering me, despite my looming mountain of self-doubt.

In the year that I'd been doing my show, WCLV and I developed the usual sponsor/broadcaster relationship. I figured when *they* told me I was good, it was mostly because my boss was helping to pay their rent. But I *had* gotten some fan mail, and from the second Conrad challenged me ("Everyone else is scared."), I knew I would do it. It was destiny. Or something.

The day of the interview I arrived at Cleveland Hopkins Airport to greet "Lenny," as he would insist that I (and everyone else) call him. I didn't know that the Maestro's contract specifically stipulated: No interviews of any kind. I just sat myself down contentedly in a convenient conference room behind the microphone and waited for Bernstein's plane to arrive from La Guardia. When he strode through the door at the head of a squadron of camel-hair coats, I greeted the charming*issimo* cultural cyclone, then in his mid-forties, and innocently invited him to sit down.

Forty-five minutes flew by as we chatted amiably about music, love, and life, and his entourage cooled their heels. Any nervousness I had quickly vanished as I found myself diving into a conversation I had unknowingly been preparing myself to have for years. The questions flowed gracefully, and my deep personal interest kept me poised on the razor's edge of his responses. When we finished, he invited me for drinks. The resulting interview got me the job of Intermission Host on the startup *Cleveland Orchestra Concerts* series, and began a life in media and the arts.

The Bernstein interview was a success for two inextricably related reasons:

1) *I was prepared.*

Though I'd never conducted an interview before, I knew my subject's work and had featured and reviewed his newest releases on my radio show. I'd also listened to most of his own serious symphonic compositions, as well as his recordings of the standard classical repertoire.

2) *I listened.*

I had the right attitude. I loved my subject, and because I was prepared, and—therefore—confident, I didn't hesitate to go deep with someone I considered to be the most brilliant man in classical music. I realized, as he started to answer my first question, that *I can do this!* I was then able to be totally present to what he was saying, which he recognized and responded to.

This poised position allows for something to take place that, for all intents and purposes, is invisible, and yet anyone who hears the result can sense. For me it happened first by sheer grace, because I happened to have both the preparation and the desire and ability to listen in this particular situation. Without knowing it, I had assumed the proper role of the interviewer.

With practice, I was able to recreate the dynamics of this graceful situation many times over, by utilizing the same principles of preparation and listening. I propose that this process can be studied and developed to enhance your abilities as an artful interviewer.

2

The Interview Concept

in'ter vyoo'

The word *interview* has its origins in two Latin words: *inter* ("between" or "among") and *videre* ("to see"). Combining them we get "a mutual view," or "reciprocal sharing of views." The French added yet another nuance to their word *entrevue*—"to have a glimpse," or "see partially." Today we most commonly use *interview* to mean any exchange of questions and answers, whether for simple obtaining of information, as in a job interview; for the official record, as in a police interview; or, more relevant to our purposes, for print or broadcast, as in a journalistic interview.

It is for this specific purpose that I propose this working definition, which has helped me conduct a range of interviews over many years:

Interview: a *mutual* process by which a skilled practitioner extracts through conversation personal, professional, or other data from an individual that will be *useful* and *interesting* to an *audience*.

Interviews are necessarily briefly opened windows that allow us only "to have a glimpse," or "to see partially." So we must always be conscious of the need to be concise, and allow as much of the picture as possible to be seen in a medium where less is more, and usually quite expensive.

But the key word in our working definition is *mutual*. To become a mutual or reciprocal sharing of views, however brief, an interview cannot simply be a quick series of questions and answers. There must be acute attentiveness, the highest level of sensitivity, and human connection.

The First Interviewer

I have a friend who is a veteran investigative journalist and filmmaker in London. He tells me that, in the opinion of British media circles, America's only major contribution to world journalism is the one-on-one interview. This may be true for broadcast media, but in print there is a much earlier predecessor to Edward R. Murrow: the timeless truth-seeker, Socrates, who died still posing questions.

In the 5th Century B.C., the philosopher Plato brought to Western thought a brilliant new form, known as the Socratic method. Plato claimed to have merely recorded a series of conversations that his master, Socrates, had conducted with various friends and pupils. Most of these talks, or "dialogues," were what we would call interviews, with Socrates as the perfect interviewer.

Before Socrates, philosophy was essentially religion, practiced by self-proclaimed wise men, whose social role was to expound unilateral (often official) versions of "the truth." Socrates, too, was interested in truth. But his approach was revolutionary: he had no answers, only questions. He was a philosopher, "a lover of ideas," especially the ideas of others, for they gave him a platform to lead an astounding series of dialogues simply by posing the right questions. Stitch by surgical stitch, his case was sewn up for him by the answers he elicited. He listened, never missing a detail. His questions illuminated the situation and the reality around it, clarifying the workings of the cosmos while straightening out the minds of the mundane.

At the heart of Socrates' search for truth was his role as "midwife" to the truth in his dialogues with others. By claiming not to have knowledge himself, his questions of others served as catalyst for answers to come. He attributed the often astonishingly profound revelations not to his own sly queries, but to the will of God acting through the dialogue. These extended interviews, some of them having more than one interviewee, or subject, follow the development of a line of thought. As one speaker finishes, Socrates asks a follow-up question, which in turn is answered, which engenders further comment, until we feel that the conversation has climbed some mental staircase up to truth itself.

Like its ancient model, the modern interview can demonstrate the same principles. You may come out of your session with a tape that satisfies the divine curiosity of the Socratic method, as well as Joseph Campbell's definition of heroism by winning something of value to bring back for the common good. And you may even have the pinnacle human experience of connection. By preparing, listening, and asking thoughtful questions, you will have enriched your audience, advanced your own learning—and perhaps recorded something that will be useful for those to come.

The Quest of the Interviewer

Quest and *question* have the same Latin root—*quaerere*: to seek, to inquire. In his classic *Hero with a Thousand Faces* (1948), Joseph Campbell charts the course of the definitive Heroic Journey. To be a hero, one's voyage must include:

- Accepting the challenge of "The Call to Adventure."
- Traveling great distances (within or without) on "The Road of Trials."
- Winning something of value to bring back for the common good.

This final point is absolutely essential: the creation of *value for others*. Not a chalice-on-the-mantle, not a sword-from-the-stone, but a gift of insight, a liberation of information—a light shed on the essence of the situation.

There are several attitudes or positions you as interviewer may take that can aid in this process. From the hard-nosed Q&A man to the sympathetic shoulder, there are many roles you will be called upon to play to facilitate the most revealing exchange possible. These roles run concurrently with the ultimate aims of the interview as "midwife" to the truth. Sometimes the truth is born feet first, kicking before it screams, sometimes smiling and glowing in gold. Sometimes it takes a scalpel. But your bedside manner has a lot to do with how the labor goes. Depending on what's needed, you can take a position objectively—withholding judgment, playing along as a partner, getting inside your subject's skin and seeing through their eyes.

To Practice Non-Judgment

No matter how well an actor prepares, he or she must remain open to the director, the other actors, the audience, to the moment. So too must the interviewer. Don't make up your mind in advance. No matter what your expectations are (and you can't avoid forming them), you must leave one variable unquantified: the subject himself or herself. You may be totally surprised and confounded. A notoriously negative subject may be in a good mood, or your energy may spark a rare positive outpouring.

In the early '90s a partner and I were developing a film for American Playhouse and Channel Four in London, about the infamous 1985 Philadelphia police attack on MOVE—a predominantly black, revolutionary, urban commune. Eleven people were killed (including five children), and two blocks of middle-class black homes were destroyed by fire when police dropped a bomb on the MOVE house and let the fire burn, leaving hundreds homeless. My partner was a long-time social activist who had already made a documentary on the group.

We'd signed Whoopi Goldberg to star as Ramona Africa, the sole adult survivor of the bombing, and were trying to write a screenplay as close to the truth as possible. In order to ensure authenticity it was necessary for us to interview numerous MOVE members in various secluded prisons in the Pennsylvania mountains.

One of the key interviews was to be with Delbert Africa, a former Black Panther Party member, who had been held in the "hole" for a number of years for refusing to allow his dreadlocks (a MOVE emblem) to be shorn, as prison regulations required. I'd seen the documentary footage of Delbert's fiery verbal assaults on Philadelphia's mayor, Rizzo, and a riot-equipped SWAT team dragging him by the dreadlocks and clubbing his head, over and over.

We arrived at the men's penitentiary in the oppressive heat of an August afternoon, the air drenched and stale. We presented ourselves at the guard gate, were searched and admitted. As they ushered us into the main lockup I realized we were walking through a large cage with thousands of men, most of color. Two little white people—one of them an attractive woman—one guard, and all that heat.

We headed toward the elevator, my partner drawing longing looks and constrained expressions of admiration from the population, many of whom walked freely about the main floor, while other prisoners gazed from the tiers of cellblocks above. The guard pushed the "down" button.

My partner had "been there before," and was admirably relaxed, but by the time we reached the subbasement I was wishing we'd stayed home. And, I thought, my mind racing as we were ushered through a series of locked gates, the worst is still ahead—an angry black revolutionary, enraged by his years of dungeon existence down here in this hellhole. What could I say to a man who'd paid such a price for his beliefs? What could I expect *him* to say?

We turned a corner and into a brick hallway with a small white room at the end. There, leaning against a pole, his dreadlocks spilling down his back, was Delbert Africa. Well, here goes nothing.

Yet as we got closer, anger and resentment were totally absent from the well-muscled and attractive young man's demeanor. All we could see was this giant smile, radiating good feeling and welcome.

"Come on in, y'all. Good to see ya."

"You got one hour," said the guard as he locked the door behind us.

The interview was not only an unqualified success, but a profound lesson for me. Delbert had taught himself to feel good despite what his conditions might be. He gave us what we needed—the historical details necessary to optimize the accuracy of the film—and much more.

As the 60-minute cassette ran out, I heaved a deep sigh of relief. Our hour was up. Yet no guard appeared. We had a few more questions, so I put in a second cassette. Delbert gladly carried on recounting stories of the internal workings of the Panthers, as well as offering personal details of his life we wouldn't dare to have asked. Another half hour passed. I flipped the cassette over, and Delbert went on. It was as if his attitude had suspended time, or, at least the repressive forces of prison regulations.

When the guard returned, he too was smiling. We thanked Delbert and floated back to our rental car. I was transformed. What had started as an attempt to simply overcome my fears had ended with a profound experience of the validity of the stance of non-judgment.

To Accompany

As a pianist who has played extensively for modern dance and opera, I have a special fondness for the role of accompanist. It is on the one hand supportive and responsive, and on the other hand sublimely powerful and directive. To sit in the accompanist's seat—in music or interviewing—you must be sensitive to both aspects.

A perfect example of this mastery is Norman Simmons, a bebop pianist, known as one of the best accompanist of singers in jazz. Before becoming permanent accompanist for master jazz singer Joe Williams, Mr. Simmons had played with a veritable Thrushes' Hall of Fame: Dakota Staton, Carmen McCrea, Anita O'Day, and Betty Carter.

In an interview aired on National Public Radio's *Jazz Profiles*, Simmons explained:

> You have to penetrate a singer's psyche. On any given day they may feel differently about a song. Your job is to intuit what their emotional state is and match it through the medium of the one constant in the equation: the song itself.

So too an interviewer must "read" his or her subject. Armed with some knowledge of the subject's work (as Simmons mastered his singers' repertoires), the interviewer intuits how the interviewee is feeling that day, the thoughts at work in their mind, what shape their physical body is in, and how all three of these things relate to the current state of their work or art. The art and the artist are connected. Your job is to reveal those connections—links the subject or the audience may not have realized themselves.

The late Joe Williams said of Norman Simmons:

> We always improvised, every night every song was different—the order, the tempo, the phrasing. Everything. Norman and I had total mutual trust, so I could just do what I felt.

This trust is the key to the interview. Without it the subject will be guarded, and your attempts to penetrate to his/her creative/psychic/experiential nexus will be blunted. Knowing your subject is the beginning of establishing that trust.

To Connect

From the interviewer's observational post, you'll find that the heart of your subject is in what they are feeling. Open up your own feelings to those of your subject, and you're navigation of their inner experience will be much more accurate than it would by using pure mental force.

I once was producing a pilot for a proposed PBS series called *Singer/Songwriter*. I was also the host, so I had the opportunity to interview a man whose music I had always loved, Randy Newman. It was a long taping, on a tiny West L.A. soundstage, and Randy had already played and sung 12 songs for our cameras, including the brilliant new novelty, "Short People," which was just about to be released. Then, he'd good-naturedly put up with me pestering him with questions about how he composed, demonstrating as we sat side-by-side at the keyboard. It was great fun, and the music had melted any ice that might have been there. When it came time for the final set-up, a sit-down one-on-one interview, it was already late at night, and I could hear his manager's grumbling impatience over the intercom from the control room.

So I tried to make every one of my questions count, and cover all the material I, as producer, needed for the finished show, without sounding perfunctory and by-the-numbers. All went well. I asked every question on my list. For all intents and purposes we were finished, and Randy looked at me for the okay to get up and leave. But tape was still rolling, and so was I.

"As a young man, your eye was permanently damaged in a car accident. What effect, if any, did that have on your life and work?"

Randy fixed me with a strange look. "Well, it made judging fly balls a little iffy," he said, laughing nervously as he lifted both hands like an outfielder, flapping them erratically. He glanced sidelong at me with a "Now are we finished?" look.

I was imagining him as a young man, sidelined on the field, recalling my own torturous adolescence, where I doled out at least as much as I received. The sound of "Short People" still ringing in my ears . . . "Did it . . . make you . . . sensitive to the pain in other people?" I watched Randy sit there immobile. I heard one of the longest, deadliest silences in broadcast history.

Then, lips still tightly compressed, he began slowly to nod his head. Was he going to get up and hit me?

"Yeah," he said, still nodding slowly, "I guess. Guilty as charged."

We froze frame and rolled credits.

3

Preparation

It usually takes more than three weeks to prepare a good impromptu speech.
—Mark Twain

People only see what they are prepared to see.
—Ralph Waldo Emerson

Abandon all hope, all ye who approach the interview without serious preparation. First of all, it's impolite, and you must use interviewer's etiquette. Secondly, it guarantees inferior results. This chapter shows you how to be prepared.

"What difference does it make?" you may ask. "I just got the assignment to interview flood victims. Big yawn! I'll just ask them, *How does it feel to lose everything?* and let the field producer and the editor handle it from there." Or your class is assigned to write a paper on your family's background, and you figure, "I'll just say, *Where were you born, Uncle Enzo?* and fake it from there." And, there's no arguing with this approach. Sometimes even the best interviewers are forced, by time and circumstance, to resort to such emergency measures. But that's what they are. Fallback positions. Plans B.

Seasoned professionals have years of experience on their sides—something to fall back on. Still, if you ask them, they'll say they use this run-and-gun approach only as a last resort; they are forced to extemporize only when all else fails. In the long run, your lack of preparation will betray you. Maybe even in the short run.

Even if you have no interest except in your own career, listen up. The prize goes to the most diligent. Even if you only know the barest rudiments of interview technique—or are already as great a schmoozer as Larry King—your boss, teacher—and most importantly—the audience will recognize an inferior product that comes from the lack of preparation. Even if you get to ask only one question, it should be the question that leads to the heart of the matter.

An Interviewer Prepares

The great Soviet theater director, actor, and producer Konstantin Stanislavski (1863-1938) literally wrote the book on preparation. In *An Actor Prepares*, his classic 1936 monograph on acting technique, Stanislavski defines the worst thing that can be said about an actor's performance: "I do not believe you." In interviewing you are playing a role as well, and the loss of credibility must be avoided. *Talent* is a prerequisite for getting the job, but *preparation* is required to keep it.

Consider the alternative: A brilliant young friend of mine, a very talented writer and editor, well-versed in spoken Spanish, recently approached an interview with Orlando Cepeda without doing the necessary research. He was in production at his magazine and got a call that the great Latino slugger was available, and he took his shot. But being young, as well as not having played baseball, my friend had nothing to fall back upon when the Hall of Famer, sensing his ignorance, began to huff and puff.

Not everyone will blow your cover, of course. In this media-savvy age, most public figures, upon achieving a certain earning-power, are awarded the famous celebrity "bubble." Encased in hermetically sealed envelopes of PR and legal sycophancy, they glide through life untouched by the demands of the real world, such as spontaneous responses to interviewers' questions. They have been supplied a short list of "talking points" and the careful rehearsal that lets them turn interviews into press releases by answering with prepared statements or sports clichés, like "There's no 'I' in team . . ." or "I just hung in there and got lucky out there . . ."

But the great Cepeda was made of sterner stuff and, feeling extremely dissed by my friend's ignorance of his career accomplishments (11 times an all-star, National League MVP, three World Series appearances, 1999 electee to the Baseball Hall of Fame) and their importance to the body of human knowledge, launched an attack that ended the interview and wasted the time and energy of all concerned.

A quick trip to the Internet and a click on any of the major search engines would have quickly divulged these heroic accomplishments, as well as the fact that the Ponce, Puerto Rico, native had been arrested in an airport on charges of attempting to pick up 160 pounds of marijuana, and sentenced to five years in state prison, of which he served ten months.

But, despite his superior intelligence, Ivy League education, street smarts, and extremely broad life-experience for one so young, my friend's failure to do his homework guaranteed humiliation and defeat.

Who, What, When, Where, Why, Etc.

Consider the journalistic Who, What, When, Where, Why, and How. You usually see this in reference to what you're supposed to cover in an investigative story. But it can also be used as a skeleton structure for how to prepare for the interview itself.

Who is your subject? Do a short biographical sketch to begin with, detailing where they're from, where they were schooled, what their cultural background is, what their aspirations were, and are currently. You should know their life well enough to be able to relate your questions and their answers to its context. The remaining unknowns can become the seeds of your questions.

What is your assignment? *What* are you supposed to be bringing back? An hour of usable dialogue? A sound bite for a lead in to a news segment? Make sure you have clearly defined the expectations for the interview before you finalize your plans. This will save you from situations like lack of resources, or a confused subject.

Most people you'll want to interview will be at least as busy as you are. Make sure your scheduling is impeccable, coordinating with your subject, your crew, and your deadlines, so that the *When* of your interview is the same for everyone involved.

Where is the interview taking place? Establish all directions beforehand, including traffic conditions or commuter times, as well as location characteristics such as noise levels, crowdedness, electricity, lighting, etc.

Why am I doing this interview? A simple question, but its answer is complex, taking us into the realms of philosophy, economics, psychology, and beyond. You'll need to answer this question on several levels at different times. You shouldn't question your chosen profession every time you prepare for an interview; if you're doing this you should probably choose another line of work. But, since the answers to this fundamental question are shaping your expectations for this interview (and, ultimately, your career), let's break it down into its components.

The more mundane level of the question is the one you'll be facing every time you step up to the mic. Asking "why" at the level of "what is expected?" and "what do I hope for?" can be very helpful in developing your interview questions and establishing your own agenda for the event.

How is the important practical consideration. How am I getting there? How is it being arranged? How is it being recorded? In short: How is this interview going to happen? What are the practical things that must occur for me to complete the assignment?

A quick run-through visualization can help this process. Soon it may become rote, but you will save yourself and the others involved innumerable headaches by making sure your "planning ahead" is actually heading in the right direction.

The Assignment

Once you've answered these basic questions, you should write everything down in a format that is usable to you and all other parties concerned. Your documentation of the interview can provide a great deal of helpful facts for future assignments, and leave you a paper trail to follow when things have gotten complicated or hazy.

Write down:
+ Subject
+ Topic
+ Date
+ Location
+ Medium
+ Expectations

When you've detailed these aspects, you'll be ready to approach the work of implementation: research and practical arrangements that will optimize your chances of realizing your goals, fulfilling your assignment, advancing your career, your quest for truth, or all of the above.

Spin

If you're a fan of old movies, you may remember newspaper reporters in films like *The Front Page*, asking their editor, "What's the angle, Chief?" or even pitching an editor a new angle to keep a dying story alive. Today this is commonly understood as "spin," and has become a household word.

The question in most corporate media today is not whether stories (and the audio, video, or print interviews they use as inserts) have been "spun," but what the spin is and how, if possible, to spin the spin itself. So if your job is to interview author Joan Didion for *The Los Angeles Times* about the journalistic "agreement to overlook the observable," or to question returning hostages for CBS, you may be handed the slant (pre-spun spin) with the job. In a particularly odious example of such an assignment, I was once hired to interview jazz piano god Bill Evans on the topic of his relationship to "rock 'n' roll."

Even supposed "alternative" media these days tend to interview almost exclusively whoever's hot, and promote the film, CD, or TV series that made them celebrity du jour. And in print media you just might find a series of full-page color pictures in the magazines that publish the interview, along with, oh yes, a large paid ad.

This happens routinely in mainstream media, with the stars of a network's new sitcoms popping up on the same network's talk shows (and, even worse, news shows) to promote their new series. This is a hallowed tradition in commercial media, to engage in commerce, by using thinly disguised infomercials to flog a new media whatever. But it can serve a higher purpose, by giving valuable background information about people of momentary prominence, the very particles of the cultural element. And, it just may provide a window (subtle, and hidden behind a lot of hype) on what the truth about the person might be.

Even if you're straight-jacketed by the spinmeisters, be the best mental patient you can be. Open a new avenue of approach. Counter spin. Reverse english. Phrase your questions as deftly as you can. Know your subject so well that your mere ultra-credible presence will evoke a breakthrough insight, forgotten fact, or relevant detail.

This is not to say that valuable opportunities for high-quality interviews have, through corporate domination, ceased to exist. This process has given us excellent in-depth interviews on shows like Bravo's unique and insightful *Inside the Actors Studio* with James Lipton, PBS's informative *Charlie Rose*, and even Comedy Central's original, often-provocative *Politically Incorrect*. Many of the rockumentaries on MTV and VH-1 have presented excellent off-network interview opportunities, as have cable networks like E!, Lifetime, and A&E. These shows are not necessarily "spinless" but they tend to be quite artful about the process, using a fine photographer's sense of what angles will be most revealing.

Radio and print are even more open to alternative spin. National Public Radio has offered *Fresh Air* and *Performance Today* and many other shows that range far beyond the reach of commercial radio in interview opportunities as well as depth of coverage. Pacifica Network, though limited in its audience, and economic and political struggles, has offered even broader opportunities, and is one of the few networks (along with the burgeoning religious broadcasters) to acknowledge its bias or spin.

In print, there is a never-ending proliferation of local and national papers, magazines, and journals that, by their very natures, offer the widest range of interview opportunities, from *The Nation* or *Z Magazine* on the Left to *National Review* and *Soldier of Fortune* on the Right. Every day, it seems, the ranks of local papers are joined by community and micro-target marketed special-interest publications, which continue to multiply as quickly as cable channels.

On the Internet, an apparent infinity of opportunities exists. Strictly speaking, every chat room is an interview of sorts. The audience is limited, but the foundation is there—already a plenitude of Net interview "shows" have spread across the cyberscape. The quality of these chats should increase as the sensorial experience of the Net develops.

Faster connections, streaming real-time audio and video, and refinement of chat room functionality will make for highly specialized, largely unlimited dialogue on every topic of human interest.

But spin or no spin, all of these interviews will require some sort of focus. Your assignment editor will, at the very least, make suggestions. Even if you're not crammed into a cubbyhole, you will be expected to focus on some particular aspects of your subject's life, work, or newsworthiness. It is in your interest to do whatever you can preemptively ("proactively" to the buzzword-inclined) to supply your own version of this point of view, angle, or approach voluntarily.

Other Limits: Prohibitions

Now that you've assessed the spin, you're ready to do the work. You know what's expected—what you need to bring back to camp after the hunt, as it were. But there is still one more consideration: What needs to be omitted? Based on the agreements that you've made, what are the limits of your interview?

In the late '80s I was producing, as well as hosting, the *Singer/Songwriter* show, which New York's WNET was piloting for PBS. The intimate one-on-one show featured solo performances by the guest as well as segments with the guest and me sitting at the piano and exploring the composition process together at the keyboard.

We'd already shot a fine show with Randy Newman and were in preproduction to tape Stephen Stills, when word came from his "people" that the admired guitarist/songwriter/singer in Buffalo Springfield and Crosby, Stills, Nash (& Young) was refusing to perform any of CSN&Y's material—even the songs he'd written for the group.

Since I was producer, the decision whether to cancel or go ahead was mine. I consulted my ascending colon and decided it was too good an opportunity to pass up. I had interviewed Stephen before at his house and liked him despite his brusqueness, and had always loved his writing and guitar heroics, so I gave the green light.

I could handle him, I figured. I was experienced with this kind of posturing. Once I was told that director Martin Scorsese would only discuss his current film *The Last Waltz*, but in my interview with him, he ended up discoursing at length on rock music, film history, his other films, and his childhood. So, I figured maybe I could similarly inspire the recalcitrant Stills.

The taping was a nightmare. For openers it was the second taping of a very long day. For reasons of economy I'd decided to shoot two shows in one tape-day, using the same crew, location, and set-up, thus saving precious thousands. Before Stephen I'd already exhausted most of my psychic energy that afternoon trying to extract dialogue from the reticent Australian singer/songwriter Peter Allen. Apparently he saved most of his creative juices for his crowd-pleasing performances. Ultimately, we were satisfied with the outcome, but it took Herculean efforts from us all. As a result the taping ran a couple of hours long, eating up the afternoon we'd set aside to plan for Stills. We were still recovering our composure when Stephen came charging through the front door, guitar already in hand, and up onto our homey little set.

"Let's go," he panted. I looked long and hard at our young director, took a deep breath, and grabbed my notes. "Ready," I answered, and went back onto the stage. For some reason (use your imagination) Stephen was wired for sound. He'd blast through one amazing tune and run out and down the hall. A pause. Then back he'd roar, up on stage for another tune, never communicating with anyone. I asked him about doing some Crosby, Stills, Nash & Young material or Buffalo Springfield—he scorched me with an evil stare and drowned me in feedback.

But the music he did give us was phenomenal. Songs from his solo albums all rendered *blues allegro agitato*. The three cameramen and I were all digging it. Our director shouted, "Great!" through the intercom after each song. What the heck, I figured. Stand back and watch.

And miraculously, when it came to the interview session, he was a different person. Sitting next to me, holding an acoustic guitar on his lap and punctuating each answer with a riff or two, he was warm and open. But I never worked harder in my life. I was smiling, nodding, throwing questions and responses, trying to keep up with this ball of fire, while the cameras hung in for dear life. When it was over I was totally fried, but we had a great show in the can.

20 Questions

On rare occasions you may actually be required to submit in advance a list of your intended questions. My advice is always to comply. For one thing, you can always ask follow-up questions that lead wherever you choose to take them. And secondly, the request for prior approval usually means that your subject is nervous, inexperienced, or both. Documentarians will encounter this stipulation fairly often.

Sometimes it's just a verbal assurance that you'll stick to a particular subject. Questions will often be requested of a biographer approaching the children of deceased artists or public figures, witnesses to historic events, or students interviewing a grandparent or community resource. One guesses *Talk* magazine complied to get Hillary Clinton.

Submitting questions is an act of good faith. It can be either a deal-breaker or door-opener. You may have no choice. I'm not counseling deceit when I strongly advise you to seize your chance, even if it means some compromise.

You can look upon this situation as an opportunity to establish trust between yourself and your subject. Your willingness to be open can go a long way toward putting your subject at ease about what to expect, and allows them a chance to prepare just as you have done. This works much better than making a demand for your creative license and journalistic freedoms. The press may be free, but the ride isn't. So I am advising that, unless you have a very specific assignment that is precluded by the prior approval process, and/or a prohibitive expense of time and money in research, travel, or facilities, walk through that door every time!

On Location

Location interviews are tricky. Sometimes, for example, a publicist tells you: "Okay. You can interview Mr. Gates but only before his dentist appointment, in the waiting room." Tricky. You'd think you'd be willing to go anywhere to interview some subjects, but always ask your contact a few questions:

Will the physical conditions be adequate?

- ◆ Light?
- ◆ Wind noise?
- ◆ Surf rumble?
- ◆ A/C buzz or other inappropriate audible intrusions?

Will your interview be the main event—or will he or she be occupied with other matters as well—in make-up, other band members wisecracking in the background, during a photo session, taking batting practice? Will it actually be a press conference?, etc.

These are important factors to ascertain in advance. Not that any one factor alone should necessarily dissuade you. It may be your job to tally the elements plus and minus. Then make a decision on a case-by-case basis. Remember, though, if you bend over backwards to interview Elton John in the studio while he's, let's say, mixing his next CD, and he senses your desperation, you may get treated like a manicurist. It's important to retain as much dignity as possible, sometimes against heavy odds. Once you've lost your subject's respect, it is usually impossible to regain. Whatever they may think of you, you must think well enough of yourself to avoid such compromising circumstances.

That being said, it's awfully difficult to prejudge these things. Both of my interviews with Leonard Bernstein involved less than ideal conditions: the first one was done without my knowing that the Maestro's contract specifically forbade interviews of any kind. Had I known this, I might have refused the challenge that became my first interview. The second Bernstein interview was not an interview at all, until I hijacked it. My program director told me that this time the "no interviews" policy was being strictly enforced, but that I should attend his management-approved press conference.

"That's bearpoop!" I trumpeted, pawing the earth in dismay. "Forget it. I'm not going to any press conference. No way."

"Of course you are, Martin," he assured me, "but you will contrive to kidnap it . . ."

I did steal the press conference, I'm only a little ashamed to say, and it produced some very memorable tape. Hijacking a press conference is a little like taking a really extended solo when you're onstage with a jazz band. Command presence, a sense of dominance derived from higher understanding, a more worthy intent—these qualities combine to allow you to rise above the sometimes shallow waters of a normal press conference situation. If you've done your homework, and you have the wherewithal to engage the speaker, you can lead the course of the discussion where you want it to go. Proof that there's always a way, *if you can but find it.*

The Downside

However . . . a few years later I decided to take a similar chance and interview pop genius Stevie Wonder at lunch at the Four Seasons. I hired an engineer to be sure that Stevie's voice was sufficiently distinct amidst the clatter of expensive silverware, china, and tuxedoed waiters. I wanted to ensure that my anticipated talk with a man I'd always cherished would be heard.

When the technician and I arrived at the table, he tried various positions for the mic stand, but none provided sufficient proximity to Mr. Wonder's mouth to be consistently intelligible, especially since Stevie's "blindisms" included a range of head motions that rendered predicting the trajectory of his voice-path virtually impossible.

He kept moving the mic stand, repositioning the boom, circling the table in search of a solution, while busy servers scampered by him. By now it was time to roll tape. I gave my colleague the let's go sign and saw him take a small table stand from his Adidas bag and place it directly in front of Mr. Wonder's plate.

Nothing would make me happier than to report that all went well. And I did do an acceptable job of yelling over the general din. But the mic planted on the tabletop brilliantly recorded the sound of every bump, jolt, moved chair, banged elbow and knee, and a myriad other collisions with the lunch table that became acoustic events so annoying that my New York producers deemed the interview unusable, and me unpayable despite my considerable exertions.

So, as far as deciding whether to venture forth to a location, be guided by my great grandmother's maxim:

Sometimes you eat the bear; sometimes the bear eats you.

A weird location can work in your favor—the authenticity of locale, the sounds, or the scenery can add visual or audio ambiance that frames your interview perfectly. Sometimes you have no choice but to go where the action is, so you get the ambiance whether you want it or not. The authenticity in these cases can be utilized with a little creativity—reference it. Make it a part of the plot. Talk about the helicopters, mention the gale-force winds, narrate the dodging of tomatoes.

For political and news/public affairs investigative reporting, some-times the only way you can get a comment from some well-protected government or business figure is by popping up unexpectedly at a public forum, stockholder's meeting, or the subject's own private office. Good examples of this can be found in virtually anything by Michael Moore, whose documentary films *Bowling for Columbine* and *Roger & Me* have taken in-the-face interviewing to the big screen. Also check out the radio program *Democracy Now!* and Amy Goodman's nothing-short-of-miraculous running interviews with fleeing govern-ment functionaries.

This is more media intervention than an interview as such, though we get some of the best insights from these confrontational methods. They usually require a combination of daredevil and seasoned reporter to pull them off, usually veterans steeped in their subject area of jour-nalistic expertise and willing to play dangerously to get the story from often very hostile subjects. They are the opposite of paparazzi, though they are similarly bothersome to the powerful. Whereas the ubiquitous cameramen's sole criterion is celebrity, the investigative reporter wants hard facts and answers to hard questions. "Content-rich," they call it.

At Home

The easiest and safest location for interviewing is usually the subject's own home. A one-on-one in their dwelling place is an interviewer's dream. It is also, needless to say, the rarest of opportunities (unless it happens to be Hef in the Playboy mansion, for many years an annual event). Your guest is now also your host, and more likely to be more comfortable, relaxed, and intimate in familiar surroundings.

Say yes to this proposal immediately—unless the subject is known to live on his or her cell phone, take calls from his or her agent, manager, stockbroker, shrink, parents, children, and anyone else likely to make your life a living hell. This is extremely rude—and rare in my experience—but it does happen. But having floated the caveat, let's agree to jump at the opportunity to play the Edward R. Murrow role (in his famous early CBS-TV series *Person to Person*) whenever we're lucky enough to be invited in.

Being Prepared

The point of being prepared (or not) was made quite humorously during a skit on the mid-60's BBC comedy show called *Not Only . . . But Also*, starring a youthful Dudley Moore and one of the most viciously satirical talents of the century, Peter Cook. The show consisted, in large part, of "sketch interviews" with two of the wittiest men in England endlessly "interviewing" each other, in telling send-ups of the often-pompous standard BBC interview. In the sketch that illustrates our point, the interviewer, played by Peter Cook, is prepared to interview a famous poet. But because of a scheduling mix-up, he finds his guest is instead a deep-sea diver played by Dudley Moore.

"So," Cook begins, as the studio audience titters in anticipation. "how do you choose between blank or rhyming verse . . . [*grand pause*] . . . at the bottom of the ocean?"

Big laugh.

But the point is obvious. People can and will surprise you. This does not mean don't prepare. On the contrary, prepare completely and totally, but be open to listening to the other "players." Know the "music" but don't simply memorize your solo in advance and then repeat it mechanically in the session. Before, during, and after the interview: stay open. You never know what the universe will send you.

4

Practical Preparations

Once you've got your attitudes and aspirations in sync, there are a range of practical details you need to tie down.

Booking

Interviews take place for a multitude of reasons: commercial, journalistic, scholarly, or for sheer entertainment (not to mention job interviews, but that's another story). If you're reading this book, you probably already know *Why* you're hosting an interview; what you want to know is some aspect of *How*.

The first step in the practical preparation for an interview is the choice of a subject, and setting a date and time for the interview to be conducted. This is called booking. Most entertainment and many cultural broadcast organizations retain on staff a booker for this purpose, often dressed up with the title Talent Coordinator. Obviously, if you are a one-time interviewer, or work for a low-budget enterprise of some kind, you will probably need to do your own booking.

Short-Timers

If this is your one-and-only interview, or you only need to do them on rare occasions, you will have to find a path to your subject, contact him or her, make arrangements, and show up on time. This might be as simple as finding a convenient time when your grandmother is sure to be home so you can bring your Walkman by to ask her questions about her childhood in the Yucatan or Serbia or Beverly Hills.

Or it may require years and years of written correspondence to obtain a commitment from the Italian town of Busseto to obtain previously unreleased documents regarding the life of Giuseppe Verdi before interviewing his distant relatives about the great opera composer's life for your forthcoming biography. Or somewhere in between, like talking Gore Vidal's publicist into setting up an interview for local radio. In every case, the point is—it's up to you: your resources, contacts, and wiles.

Beats and Retreats

Should it become your happy lot (as it has become mine, from time to time, over the years) to obtain a job that calls for regular interviews—daily, weekly, whatever—you will find yourself developing a beat—a routine and territory to ply it in. This means more-or-less durational relationships with institutions that handle the kind of person you regularly interview: NBA Players of the Week, convicted elected officials, harpsichord players, or punk-rock roadies. There will turn out to be someone who handles their publicity. You may end up talking with this person a lot. At least as long as you both keep your jobs.

There are good things that you can make happen with a smart publicist. You will come to know the ones who want to work closely with you. Be selectively open to whatever they suggest. When you have "holes to fill" (slots to use interviews with their clients in a daily program or column), you can find a way to "trade" with some of your publicist contacts. You can help them by taking an occasional chance on one of their "almost famous" clients, in exchange for help getting "the toughies"—clients who have hired them not to *get* publicity but to *avoid* it, by gatekeeping the press at a distance. I know it sounds like a sellout, but you've committed yourself to a job that—unless you represent a high-powered journalistic entity—may entail this kind of compromise, at least tactically.

In the early '80s I was West Coast Producer for a syndicated radio show. I had developed relationships with most of the L.A. publicity firms, but there was one publicist in particular, an attractive woman in her late twenties, who had that professional "wanna dance?" look in her eyes. Her medium-sized agency had a lot of film people, so I attended her clients' screenings about once a week. And when the occasion permitted, we'd sit together in the very last row.

Anyway, I did some "vanity" interviews for her, not all of which, I must confess, made it on the air. But she said her clients were happy, and she would regularly express her gratitude, when she could, by giving me access to her A-list in return.

One time I favored her by interviewing actor Efrem Zimbalist, Jr., to publicize a new Movie-of-the-Week he was in. I can't remember what I asked him, as my friend and I sat with him on a sunny day in her ficus-rich office in West Hollywood, but, needless to say, I was ultra-polite to the aging star whom my parents had loved as suave private detective Stuart Bailey on the legendary TV series *77 Sunset Strip* (1958-1964).

I kept it respectful and brief, but when we neared the end (you always know when this is), he was bragging about his close friendship with the late FBI Director, J. Edgar Hoover. Knowing that I had enough on tape already, I blurted: "In view of the revelations that have emerged since Hoover's death regarding his behavior, have you begun to reassess you relationship with the Director?"

"Oh, no!" Mr. Zimbalist phumphered, looking genuinely shocked. "You have to remember The Director was facing perilous times. There were all these revolutionary groups out there, like The Lettermen and the SDA [sic]." And that's the part my producers aired (at my suggestion).

When they did, they left on the tape the barely suppressed giggling of my publicist friend and me. We couldn't help ourselves. Mr. Zimbalist had betrayed his woefully marginal knowledge of the radical politics of the times by botching the names of two of the '60's counterculture's most infamous groups, The Weathermen and the Students for a Democratic Society, the SDS.

Developing Your Network

It never hurts to use your friends and neighbors. This is all about people. If people *like* you (i.e., like your work) they'll be happy to recommend you to their friends. You can't live on these connections, but when they crop up, you should add them to your bag o' tricks. Soon you'll be going from recommendee to recommendee, like Tarzan swinging from vine to vine.

In the late '70s I had the good fortune to interview the stunningly beautiful Yvette Mimieux, star of *Where the Boys Are, Light in the Piazza, Toys in the Attic*, and many more. She was starring in an unfortunately forgettable film, and my publicist friend wanted the interview as a favor. I drove out to Stone Canyon Road and had an enjoyable afternoon, staring at the goddess while my Nakamichi 500 portable did the work.

When we were, alas, finished, Ms. Mimieux began to praise my interviewing savoir-faire, which I brushed off as mere hostessly politesse. "You might be the one to interview Bronny Kaper," she told me. "He doesn't usually do interviews, but I could call him . . ."

The late Bronislaw Kaper was one of our best film composers/songwriters ("On Green Dolphin Street," "Invitation," "Heigh-Lili, Heigh-Lo"—all of which became jazz standards), so I jumped at the chance. "Would you call him for me?" I asked Yvette.

"Of course," she said, and next week at his home in Beverly Hills I spent a captivating afternoon of duly-recorded conversation with Mr. Kaper, a Polish-American, who, among other things, had personally brought Roman Polanski to America. We talked about everything under the sun—from symphonic music to jazz to the origins of Eastern Bloc Stalinism. He even played "Green Dolphin Street" for me on the piano. When the time came to leave, I packed up my gear and started for the door, but couldn't resist a closer look at his German Blüthner grand piano.

Kaper followed me over to the glowing ebony instrument, and from his body language I felt encouraged to sit down to play. I lifted the piano lid and hubristically attempted Kaper's own "Heigh-Lili, Heigh-Lo," although I'd never played it before. I got only as far as the third bar before needing to ask him for the next chord. I looked imploringly up into his face. He knew what I wanted. "The way I play it, or the way Bill Evans plays it?"

If you're given a pig, bring home the bacon. Get the most out of the opportunities you're offered, however unpromising they may appear at the outset. Don't be like those foreign correspondents, who, no matter what country they're assigned to, never leave their fancy American-style hotel, but instead hang around the pool (or the bar) waiting for official government handouts. Get off your duff! Off your couch, Potato!

One of the least likely relationships I developed in my early days as a professional interviewer/West Coast correspondent for syndicated radio was with a charming, intelligent man named Heber Jensch, then Regional Director (now, I think, a Huge Honcho) for a Church of Scientology front group called National Commission on Law Enforcement and Social Justice.

This was at a time when conventional wisdom held that Scientology was a scourge of mankind second only to the Manson Family and failure to floss. But I was just starting out and hungry for leads, so I figured I'd check them out. In fact, the NCLESJ, despite its Scientology affiliation, did yeoman service in uncovering abuses by Interpol, the FBI, the CIA, and other police agencies, psychiatric institutions, and various other unsavory groups and practices then going unchecked.

Inevitably, some of the subjects Heber pitched me were self-serving, but on balance they were substantive, and a consistently high-quality relationship had been created, and by the time I moved on, they'd supplied ten or eleven usable investigative subjects for the shows I served. And I almost turned them down.

Facilities, Materials, and Crew

Having booked your guest, it is time to get down to business. Especially if you are doing this solo, or are producing as well as interviewing, you need to compile a checklist of facilities:

- Cassette or Mini-Disc recorder(s)
- Camera(s)
- Tape/film
- Microphone(s)
- Lights

- Studio; soundstage
- Editing bay; digital facilities

Tape's Cheap (Don't Leave Home Without It)

I'll never live down my interview with The Who's Peter Townshend. I was Public Service Director of pioneering "progressive" rock station WMMS-FM in Cleveland, doing a weekly interview show called *Electric Tongue*. Needless to say it hadn't been easy booking the acrobatic guitarist and acclaimed composer of the rock opera *Tommy* and most of The Who's succession of hits.

It was the first *Tommy* tour, and the band was hotter than the Rolling Stones and equally unacquainted with sobriety. I'd spent almost a week wheedling, cajoling, and threatening their American management before I got the booking.

On the morning of the interview date I figured: better take no chances; go first-class: bring an engineer to set up the mics, get audio levels, and run the tape recorder. I chose our brilliant young production director, a genius audio engineer and nth-degree Who fan. He'd even brought a professional reel-to-reel recorder. None of this cheesy cassette nonsense!

It was a pretty decent interview. I'd been warned that Townshend could be tough: if you didn't know your stuff, he would eat your liver. But, after a slow start, everything was rolling; he'd analyzed *Tommy* from a traditional operatic perspective, dealt with the question of ritual instrument-smashing, and was starting into his beliefs in music as a carrier of political and, especially, spiritual values.

I took a deep breath. *Yes! This was the deep stuff!* I relaxed and smiled at Peter, who was lost in pre-postulation answer-formation, filling our spinning reels with delicious, airable minutes of brilliant rock ideation. *Al' right!*

In triumph I looked over at my engineer, just to share the victory. I could just see us editing this material together.

But no smile from my audio man. His face was scrunched up in pain. Huh? As a reflex I looked over at the tape machine. The take-up reel was turning, flap-flap-flapping the tail-end of a tape. And the other reel was empty.

"We're out of tape," he said finally.

Townshend finished his sentence.

"So, put on a new one. Quick!" I whispered.

"I don't have one," he grunted through gritted teeth.

"What?"

"I didn't bring any more . . ."

So ended a less-than-perfect day, with me apologizing to Peter and his manager for the gaffe, while watching our embarrassed engineer literally *hurl* his equipment into carrying cases.

Know All Deadlines

- Interview date
- Editing/sweetening date
- Drop-dead delivery date
- Air date/publication deadline

Whether or not you're ultimately responsible for any or all of these details, it's good to be aware of your interview's place in time.

Transportation

Remember that transportation is an important function as well. How are you (your subject, any crew, equipment, or props) getting to and from the interview site?

The Crew

Make a list of relevant participants (with e-mail and street address; telephone/pager number; fax number); crew that you need to hire, or be responsible to:

- Director
- Camera person(s)

- Sound person
- Lighting director
- Grip(s)
- Driver
- Other

Check all details carefully. Whether it's just you or a five-camera shoot in Petaluma, one wrong number can scuttle the (otherwise) best-laid plans. A contact list is another necessity.

Contact List

- Your contact person
- Interview subject
- Subject's publicist
- Subject's manager
- Whoever (else) is responsible for booking the interview

Note what each person's wishes, needs, and/or requirements include:

- Deal memo/contract/rights agreement/release forms
- Copy of final interview/show/article
- Stills of the shoot
- Input at editing/mixing sessions
- Right of final cut

Although these may be done by your secretary, management, Legal Department, Business Affairs Department, your mother, or someone else powerful above you, they may be of extreme importance (deal-breakers), and must be handled by *somebody!*

The Fruits of Your Labors

Finally, you will go back to your research notes. These may take a number of forms. I still make longhand notes with my trusty Pentel on a yellow legal pad and entrust them to a file folder if I need to include other documentation, such as:

- Research material (hard copy)
- Downloads from the Net (highlighted for easy retrieval)
- Previous interviews (ditto)
- Newspaper or magazine articles, reviews (ditto)
- Press releases, CD liner notes

Most importantly, your notes should include the areas, concepts, or topics you may want to cover in the interview—anything from a childhood story you heard your subject tell on *Conan* to a review in *The New York Times*, your local paper, or Amazon.com to an answer your subject gave to an earlier interviewer.

These may come in handy, and will tell your subject you cared enough to do some secondary research.

Opening Question

In addition, your notes should include a potential opening question, written out so that if you panic (some subjects are scary), you can read it verbatim. Hopefully your subject's answer will be long enough for you to regain your equilibrium—and may spark your next question.

Start Where You Are

Ask yourself, "What in my own life has been like my subject's life? What do we have in common?" Simple examples range from being the same age, going to the same school, to your spending your life studying the area in which your subject excels. Some interviewers who become broadcasters, journalists, or documentarians are experts in a particular area. Some have worked in a profession and know it from the inside, like Johnnie Cochran, Terry Bradshaw, or Pat Buchanan. Others are scholars, sportswriters, financial or computer whizzes who moonlight doing broadcast or print interviewing in one form or other.

But most of us are simply people drawn to the work from the civilian ranks. Nevertheless, we must have some area of expertise, some field we love, majored in college. My first area of interest was music. I worked with a classical radio station, but I also ran a chain of record stores and had heard *South Pacific,* Satchmo, and Shostakovich in my parents' home. I am also a mediocre pianist and worse singer. But I love all kinds of music, and that's where I was, so that's where I started. But I soon spread to writers, political figures, filmmakers—anyone with whom I could find common ground.

What is your background? Start there. If you're just starting out, use what you have. If you're a seasoned journalist, try to dig into your own life experience, as efficiently as you can, as deep background for your work.

Time: The Key Element

Before we explore the techniques of hosting the interview itself, let's remember the most important single consideration in shaping an interview for whatever medium—time.

- ◆ How much time (or column space) is the interview expected to fill?
- ◆ How long do you have to do the interview?
- ◆ How long do you have to edit it?
- ◆ Keep a stopwatch at hand, or locate the studio clock and (subtly) keep a sharp eye on it.

Even the briefest meditation on the nature of time will tell you why:

As world-famous linguistics expert Noam Chomsky aptly reminds us, the time allotted for questions and answers necessarily limits the content of the interview. Some things are more complicated than others. Any complex issue deserves a suitable period of time to explore its history, dynamics, context, and ramifications. Soundbites preclude all of this, by simply excluding any real discussion—only a tiny unilateral fragment of the issue in question.

However, in real life you may not be afforded enough time to allow your guest to unspool a complete geopolitical history of Honduras for you in order to explain a current event.

You may not have time to take the "layers of the onion" approach to explore with Placido Domingo exactly how a Spanish singer becomes an Italian tenor. Or a point-by-point analysis by Shaquille O'Neal on how his growth pattern shaped his ego structure.

So, determining the size of the envelope will allow you to judge how much you can stuff into it. And how fast. Knowing your time-frame lets you structure your questions to gain maximum content per minute. Even if you're going directly "to tape" and have the luxury of cutting later, it's always a good idea to compress your question to fit the time frame. Ask any editor.

I learned from years of editing my own shows with a razor blade that less is more. Only an ill-prepared interviewer allows his subject to over-talk, to ramble, to slip out of focus. The better you structure your questions, the more succinct your subject's answers. Even if he or she ad-libs a story, a joke, a free-association leading to an important personal revelation or psychic breakthrough, the way you've structured your time will encourage your guest to economize verbally.

A lot of this will depend on your attitude.

5

The Interview Attitude

One person seeks a midwife for his thoughts;
the other, someone he can assist.
Here is the origin of a good conversation.
—Friedrich Nietzsche, *Beyond Good and Evil*

If you've done your preparation well, you've already got the right posture to do a great interview: The Student of Life. Realize that you are among nature's chosen few to be working as an interviewer in the first place, for one fundamental reason: here is a golden opportunity to continue your education at someone else's expense, and get paid for it. (Or maybe not.)

So, be happy. Happy you've done your preparation and been turned on to something new: memories of your grandfather's village, Steve Earle's new CD, Steve Soderbergh's new movie, Walter Moseley's new book, a proposed plan for civic improvement, something to feed your brain on your journey of lifelong learning.

This is the *only* attitude.

Choose a Role: Everyman, the Director, and/or the Fan

Although there is only one attitude toward interviewing, a combination of joy and gratitude, there are a number of roles, or characters, an interviewer must play, consciously or not. These roles are determined by three factors: your assignment, your experience/ability, and your interview subject. In actuality, most interviews turn out to be an ad hoc blend of all three. But the points of view, and resulting techniques of each of these roles, are essentially different, so we should study them separately.

Everyman (Disciple/Master)

The most basic role an interviewer should play is audience representative. You are Everyperson. Tribune of the people. Most people would like a crack at questioning Johnny Depp, Dick Cheney, Phil Jackson, Venus Williams, or Joshua Bell. But only few are chosen—in this case, you. So be a faithful surrogate; ask the questions you think the audience wants answered, even if they don't know it yet. Ultimately your success as an interviewer will depend on customer satisfaction, whether the audience feels it receives full value from the answers your questions evoke. When participatory democracy actually works, it does so because our elected representatives take their responsibilities seriously. Go Thou and do likewise.

The everyman role takes you, as an individual, out of the equation, thus avoiding whatever personality clashes or ego battles might result from a more personalist approach.

Here are typical everyman questions through which you speak for members of your audience:

- Questions that begin, "Tell us why . . .?" (in which the "us" refers to the implied audience; or
- "How do you respond to people who say . . .?" in which you separate yourself out from the churls who might ask such a provocative question; or, alternatively . . .
- "Critics have said . . ." or still
- "On the other hand, isn't it true that . . ."

Another way of approaching this same role is as a student chosen to represent your class. In many Asian cultures learning is transmitted through the master/disciple relationship. Although this has a distinctly antidemocratic ring to it, when we understand that the master, in order to fulfill his role properly, must learn from the disciple, at the same time as imparting wisdom to him, the reciprocal nature of the relationship is made clear.

Even if you feel yourself a master—of journalism, of your chosen field of endeavor, whatever it may be—you have something to learn from your guest, so become his or her disciple for the duration of the interview. The audience will love you for accepting the humbling truth that you are there merely to help your audience learn from your guest, so the role of student is completely appropriate. Sit at your subject's feet, figuratively, or, as I did once with Gore Vidal, literally:

I thought I had to talk my program director into letting me interview distinguished American writer Gore Vidal. It was, after all, for a classical *music* station. I invoked every pretext, dodge, ruse, and canard to sway what I feared might be a closed mind. My PD let me suffer for a bit, then looked pityingly at me across his desk and said: "Martin, he's Gore Vidal."

The prolific American novelist, essayist, and dramatist was in Los Angeles promoting yet another new book on *The Tonight Show*, and a colleague, knowing my admiration for the author, had put me in touch with his publicist.

As I drove up to Vidal's secluded U.S. pied-à-terre in Outlook Estates I turned over the thesis of his new book: that the U.S. had ceased being a democracy and had become a "National Security State." There was much I agreed with in his exegesis of the American drift toward authoritarianism, but I had a few problems/questions as well. How would I proceed? I'd had almost no lead time to prepare for the interview, and had to get off the air and immediately dash through rainy Hollywood rush hour to keep the appointment. Luckily I'd read the book, and most of its predecessors.

I was met at the door of his suitably baronial Spanish Mission home by a much taller man than I'd imagined. I followed his athletically aristocratic gait into the front room, set up my equipment, and sat down on a small couch with the mic stand between us. Intending to do a number of quick back-and-forth questions and answers for my series of daily 90-second "featurettes," as the session unfolded I was increasingly confounded by Vidal's tendency to give extended lectures in response to each of my questions, without actually looking at me. Not that they were windy, tedious, or anything short of his usual brilliance. But, as he stared out his big bay window as he spoke, it was clear that I was present in the room primarily to announce the topic of his next lesson, and turn the cassette over. One can only say "uh-hunh" and "mmmm" so many times, after all.

In a flash, as he finished his second or third mini-oration, I grabbed the mic off of its stand, slid as decorously as possible off the couch onto the floor, and positioned myself *literally at the great man's feet.* This act of ritual obeisance made it easier for me simply to sit there as supplicant as he discoursed, pulling the microphone back only to ask another brief question.

It proved a stratagem of unique efficacy. Vidal was apparently pleased to have an interviewer acknowledge *physically* the superiority he assumed, *intellectually and spiritually.*

I would edit two full weeks of *Martin Perlich Interviews* from the Vidal tape. Audience reaction would be vocal and very positive. *And* the "at thy feet" humility allowed me the psychic elbowroom to ask one really incendiary question just before I stopped the tape—which I'll discuss later.

The Director

You may have heard the term "actor's director," which refers to film or stage directors who are usually actors themselves. Actors' directors like Charlie Chaplin, Orson Welles, Richard Attenborough, Robert Redford, Penny Marshall, and Ron Howard all knew what it took to coax performances out of their casts that may elude other directors.

Set yourself up off-camera (or mic), even if you insert an image or audio of yourself later. This positions your guest as an actor in a scene, for all intents and purposes, rather than a person casually engaged in conversation with another person (although this can be later edited to look like it).

In the director's posture, you are not so much asking questions as giving direction. Gently but confidently you elicit your subject's response with polite instructions such as:

"Please start that story over again, Ms. Parton, but this time begin with: 'I met Porter Wagoner . . .'"

Or

"Please frame your answers by referring to the question I asked, like, 'Being an abused child myself, I guess my books tend to deal with characters who have also had to suffer in some way.'"

Or

"Narrate for us exactly what you saw, Mr. Montana, as you dropped back to look for Jerry Rice coming free behind the cornerback . . ."

The director approach has two salient virtues:

1) Editors love it, because it gives them the guest's answer, expressed as a statement or narrative, in-the-clear, so as it can be cut into a documentary, short feature, whatever, and not sound cut-and-pastey or stepped on; and

2) Perhaps more importantly it allows you to take charge of the interview from the beginning and shape it. By taking yourself out of the picture (or off-mic) you cede preeminence to your subject, in exchange for the subtle dominance that being a director seems to confer.

The Accidental Director

There are some guests—in show business or out—who are dying to perform. You may not know this going in, but your mere entrance (with or without the presence of the camera crew) may trigger some special area in your subject's brain (or adrenal gland) that has been just lying in wait. When this happens, lay back. Luxuriate as you let the tape roll, always keeping your questions to a minimum. Unless you have time or content constraints, do not try to control the situation. Let your subject go. Sit there and laugh, if it's natural; nod your head when you agree. Like a marlin on a line, your subject will soon tire, and ultimately end up in the boat. Think of yourself as playing out the line.

This has happened to me often, especially with comics, like Jackie Mason or Martin Mull, or occasionally singers, like Lou Reed, Al Jarreau, or Jackson Browne.

Jackie Mason came up to my studio on the brink of his first come-back after allegedly giving Ed Sullivan the finger on Ed's own show. Jackie had been forced to put his career on "hold" for a number of years during the ensuing blackballing that prevented him from working the best venues.

About ten minutes before our afternoon appointment he came trundling up my studio stairs unannounced, holding out a hand for me to shake, and commenced to monologize before I had time to unwrap a new cassette. What made the task harder was that from the first word, I couldn't stop laughing; the man was that hilariously funny! Whether prepared or spontaneous material (or some combination) he got me cackling, and that was that. I simply stayed off-mic, tried to muffle my endless guffaws, and take advantage of Jackie's very few pauses to redirect the flow of the "conversation" in order to cover a certain number of required topics. It was great listening, though—(maybe because) I made almost no contribution, except the decision to chill out.

Sometimes, if you feel brave, you may be compelled to leave your imaginary director's stool and participate in the festivities. Be bold, but, by all means, be careful to remain a good host. Do not, in the rarefied air of the jam session that may ensue, step on your guest's toes. And be ready to cut OUT! If your guest wants to step up and take an extended solo—let them.

Martin Mull is a rare genius. Master of the tiny gesture (the nuanced hyperbole, you might call it), he is an American John Cleese, albeit a much better musician. When I'd interviewed him live on the air at legendary L.A. rock station KMET, his first line was "Let's swap first names" (do the math). For some reason I'd felt called upon to try to keep up with the mercurial Mull (it was, after all, my show), but I didn't know his material as well as he, and encountered more turbulence—and dead air—than I felt comfortable with.

So, a few years later when I again had the pleasure of his company, this time on tape, I was prepared to be fast on my feet, but equally happy to step back from the mic and watch.

I was far more active—provocative, you might say, with "Rock 'n' Roll Animal" Lou Reed. I was awaiting his arrival at the KMET studios, to tape my show *Electric Tongue*, when word came that Mr. Reed was instead waiting in the bar next door. Grabbing a portable machine, I jumped over to the mostly empty bar and located the elusive Velvet Underground star, set up the mic, and, propelled by the combined energies of Reed's substantial reputation as a smart-ass, my own semi-ruffled feathers, and the recent successes of the antiwar movement, I started out with a question of some impertinence:

"So, Lou, do you agree that we should pull our Dick out of Vietnam?"

"You mean Nixon?" Reed answered, not dropping a beat.

At one point I noticed the only customer in the dark mid-Wilshire watering hole, an unshaven guy in a suit, peering across the darkened bar to identify the raucous voices breaking each other up at the table in the back. I peered back and recognized a new star of NBC's *Saturday Night Live*, Bill Murray. He was laughing, too.

Lou Reed gave me wit, not music, but in the case of Al Jarreau, the extraordinary jazz singer who'd labored year after year trying to make a living on the L.A. jazz circuit (which, in the late '60s/early '70s was less than robust) and who'd finally had a crossover hit—I got both:

As I set up my equipment, a somewhat shy Mr. Jarreau expressed reluctance to discuss his long lonely years of dues-paying, and suggested a few other topics that he also felt might be too-succinct-for-audience-consumption.

I had prepared a number of questions on just these topics, but when the tape was rolling, I put my clipboard down, crossed the room to the sofa, sat down, took a deep breath and asked:

"When I hear you sing at The Baked Potato, you seem to be in direct touch with your subconscious, especially when you scat. Are you conscious of your subconscious? I don't know exactly why I asked that question, but does it make any sense to you at all?"

Al looked at me with an expression that scared me at first, then slowly became a faint smile.

"My subconscious. Yeah. Okay. Maybe so. That's where I go when I sing. Yeah, especially when I scat."

"Give us an example."

There followed one of the most delicious 45 minutes of my life as I merely sat there, in my virtual director's chair, and listened to Al Jarreau give an illustrated history of scat singing, improvising in many styles, from Oo-blah-dee to Ool-yah-koo.

Ready when you are, Mr. or Ms. . . .

The Fan

Most people are pleased to be stroked, within reason. But the road to hell is paved with fatuous flatterers. So, in order to take this third approach, that of fan, enthusiast, aficionado, scholar, expert, maven, or distant admirer, either you actually have to be one of the above or, in the process of preparation, you become one. Either way you will bring sincere enthusiasm to the interview, which, despite whatever else you lack, will register positively with your subject. Rest assured, empty butt-kissing will usually—alas, not always—do just the opposite. Certain celebrity interviewers do little else!

Better to be a real fan.

Not too long ago, when I was developing the MOVE film for American Playhouse/Channel Four in London, I met with the Executive Producer—an acclaimed BBC filmmaker, famous for mixing real people and actors to lend an air of verisimilitude to his notably socially conscious films. He was in America producing a film for Warner Bros. about the building of the first atom bomb, starring Paul Newman and John Cusack.

It was our first casting meeting, held in his office on the Warner lot. Since the main character in our film was a black woman, I put forward the name of Whoopi Goldberg, a young comic whose one-woman show for HBO had been a stunning piece of dramaturgy. Yet my British producer laughed at the suggestion, as did my partner. But I was a fan, and soldiered on. "Whoopi's the one," I told them. "Who ya got that's better?"

They thought and thought, but they could suggest no better candidate. My choice prevailed, and we set sail to sign the brilliant young actress, who, coming off *The Color Purple*, was getting hotter by the day.

Through perseverance I managed to finesse our script around her agent, manager, et al., directly to Whoopi, who actually read the script within a week and got word back to us she liked it, let's talk. Unfortunately, Whoopi couldn't meet with us before she hit the road to tour her new version of the HBO show. So . . . could we meet her in Detroit?

We appeared backstage at General Motors' Fisher Hall that night, after her brilliant new show, and presented ourselves at Whoopi's dressing-room door. My partner was polite but formal, but I couldn't help myself.

My partner looked worried. Cool it, Martin. She's right, I told myself. Just chill. Try impersonating a professional. But no, it wasn't star-struckness, celeb-worship, *paparazzo* behavior. We were in the presence of an authentic genius! A woman whose work I so greatly admired that I, despite everything, threw caution to the wind, picked up a publicity photo off a pile of glossies on her make-up table, and asked Whoopi for an autograph.

I thought my partner would crawl under the carpet. Again I doubted myself. Agonies of paranoia. But Whoopi just twinkled her famous grin, graciously autographed the photo, and we left, agreeing to come to her suite in the morning for an interview. My partner could hardly wait to start dressing me down. How unprofessional! No one acts that way. Whoopi thinks I'm a dreidel. On and on.

Next morning a gracious Whoopi Goldberg was at the door to welcome us into her penthouse suite. Tensely we took seats on her couch and began to pitch the movie. I had barely begun my spiel when she waved me to a stop, smiling, and said:

"I already know all this. Where do I sign?"

We had nothing legal prepared. "All we need is a Letter of Intent," I told her.

She walked over to the writing desk, wrote a few lines on hotel stationery, came back to the couch, and handed it to us. It read:

"I am committed to playing Ramona Africa for Karen Pomer and Martin Perlich *with all my heart and soul* (Emphasis in original) —Whoopi Goldberg."

If you *are* a fan, let yourself *be* a fan.

All of the Above

Most interviews seem to elicit a combination of some or all these roles. Feel free to mix and match. The key to role selection is what seems most comfortable and effective for all concerned. Don't be afraid of floating back and forth between the roles . . . as appropriate.

A final approach to your subject can be found in the Golden Rule, which simply and elegantly states:

Do unto others as you would have them do unto you.

As corny as it may seem, simple observation of this ancient maxim will prepare you intuitively for any interview subject. The Golden Rule in this context is a call for compassion, a commandment for you to "walk a mile" in your subject's shoes. And if you are graced with the kinesthetic leap that can be made from one mind to another, you will truly be able to experience life from their side of the story. You won't have to ask the clichéd question, "What is it like. . . ?" Because you'll know.

"At Ease!"—Offstage Pleasantries

One of the key maneuvers in interviewing is to get to know your guest before you roll tape. In some rare cases you can arrange a formal pre-taping meeting in a manager's office. More usually, you'll have an interval of undetermined length between the time your guest comes through the door (or you go through theirs) and the time you ask your opening question.

Sometimes it's easy, while you're setting up, or while the commercials are playing, or whenever, to get friendly and at the same time put your guest at ease with your intentions:

- ◆ Describe your audience
- ◆ Explain your format
- ◆ Range of questions, content, etc.
- ◆ How you'd like answers framed

Here, also, is your first chance to:

- Acknowledge your appreciation for your guest's life and work
- Display knowledge of his/her field
- Establish your role: Everyman, Director, Fan
- Put your guest at ease

Do this first, time permitting. Everyone does better work relaxed.

Now, when a guest is shown into the studio, I greet them with a sincere power gush of thanks that they've driven—on L.A. freeways—all the way to Northridge, at the northwest corner of Southern California's San Fernando Valley. I thank them in the name of the audience, whose lives they will enrich with their insights. And it's true—or I've chosen my guest unwisely. I'm always relaxed enough to be almost casual. I've done my research, have my notes, and I also carry the commitment to bring the best out of both of us, so that we're usually already pleasantly engaged as we go on the air. I read a brief bio and PR release about the subject's play, novel, film, ballet, concert, master class, reading, or exhibition—then we talk. Later, we take smiley digital pictures for our Website.

6

The Interview Itself

If you don't ask the right questions, you don't get the right answers.
A question asked in the right way often points to its own answer.
Only the inquiring mind solves problems.
—Edward Hodnett

A wise man's question contains half the answer.
—Solomon Ibn Gabirol

This is it. This is what we've been preparing for. This chapter examines the factors that make up a successful interview: any guest, any medium, any length. You've done your preparation, arrived at the site in one piece, and have the correct equipment in place. Show time.

Action!—Markers, Sticks, and Slates

Since the earliest days of silent film, during shooting, every scene, every successive take of every movie, has begun with a shot of a small blackboard on which is written in chalk: the film's name, scene, and take number. This "clapboard" (today referred to as "sticks" or "marker") allows the director to locate and identify every individual snippet of action on the many reels of film from which he and his editor will use to stitch together the finished film. When the camera has looked at the board long enough, the person holding it "claps" the (usually striped) top board (or stick) opened and closed, runs out of camera range, and the action, thus "marked," can begin.

Television

Today the boundaries between film and TV have become so blurred that, at the production level at least (and the decision to use film or digital video), they are virtually identical. If you're in the field, you can yell into your camcorder: *"Indonesian Militiaman* Take Three!" or use a slateboard or clapsticks. If you have a field producer, you won't have to worry.

Radio

In radio it is traditional to record an interview subject's name, the date, and the location at the beginning of the recording:

"Barbra Streisand; June 11, 2004, Bel Air . . . Slate."

The slate is your vestigial clapboard, your radio "marker." It tells all concerned that you're ready to begin, pay attention. It also will save your butt if "someone" forgets to label the tape, or the label is lost or obliterated. Any other editing instructions can be spoken parenthetically onto the running tape as the convenient occasion arises.

With the "marker" or "slate" out of the way, you're ready for . . . "Action!" in the form of your opening question.

The Opening Question

The Buddhists speak of the universe's endless love affair between Form and Emptiness. "Emptiness" means that until you fill the moment with the "Form" of your opening question it is empty. Fill 'er up with Supreme. Make the Form with which you fill your opener the absolute best that the moment (and all your preparation) can deliver.

Always assume your first question may be your last. Make it count. Your guest may be called away suddenly; an act of God may intervene, who knows? Front-load your interview with a killer opener. Sometimes that's all your assignment calls for:

"What is the refugee situation in Abu Dhabi?"

"Do you have a suspect in this case, Chief?"

But, more often, the opener is just that: the gateway to the heart of the subject's essence, career achievement, fighting spirit, or social vision—all riding on your first question. Consider it well.

The opener is primarily a calling card. You know who your subject is; even if you've schmoozed briefly beforehand, he or she will not "know" you. Your guest may be paddling through a series of 10 interviews a day in 15 cities. Your opener is a way to distinguish yourself from all the other media droids; bring something fresh to the travel-weary subject.

The opener speaks volumes about who you are. It should contain a kernel of original insight into the subject and his or her work. Your research and preparation should have this as a primary goal. Show that you care enough to have penetrated past the home page of their official Website. The opener should display both your power and respect for your subject.

HINT, HINT: Never ever use any question that begins:

"So . . . how did it feel . . .?"
"What was it like . . .?"

Or, my favorite biographical obfuscation:

"Where did it all begin for . . . Wynton Marsalis?" (Get ready to duck.)

Unless your subject is a flood victim or other distressed soul—or you're trolling for a soundbite—these lazy journalistic clichés can only expose you as a hack, and turn whatever you're attempting into gruel.

Be original in a respectful, understated way. With appropriate humility show yourself in the best possible light. Let your opener say: "I'm an accomplished professional who cares enough about you and your work to take both seriously. And this question shows that I have examined it and have had these unique and original responses to it."

Right

I was lucky enough to be hired to do an audio-documentary on jazz guitarist Pat Metheny, when he made his recording debut. Pat is ten years (at least) younger than I, was raised in the Plain States, and cut his musical teeth on the music of the Beatles. A brilliant player, there was something unique about his approach to playing. Something fresh. Completely devoid of the endless note-spinning and displays of "dig-me chops" much in favor among tyro jazz and "fusion" players of the day. I loved his work, so the research was a pleasure. Fan City again.

"You say in your recent interview in *Guitar Player* magazine that you never practice. Does that mean that you find practicing is an unacceptably low mode of performance and that you let your constant playing—which I understand from other musicians is typically an all-day affair—take the place of practicing?"

Pat whirled around, picked up one of his guitars and proceeded to give an impromptu demonstration of the difference between live performance and mere practicing. He held on to the instrument and, as the interview continued, he gifted us with a series of answers illuminated by signature guitar riffs, examples from his new LP, as well as amazingly lifelike approximations of the music that had influenced his style.

I had found the right opener.

Wrong

I wish I could say the same for the first question I ever asked Frank Zappa.

I'd been in L.A. all of one week, a cheeky kinda guy from the Midwest, when the Columbia Records promotion man asked me if I'd like to interview the great rock guitarist, composer, satirist, and cultural icon. Now, I was the guy who'd taken great pleasure in playing Zappa's first recording with the Mothers of Invention, *Freak Out!* on a major classical music station, so I was more than ready. The promo man said, "Hop in," so without a moment's preparation, not even the chance to take a hurried, last-second note or two, we were off.

Zappa lived in the Hollywood Hills, high atop Laurel Canyon, in a big house that was mostly studio. We went in, cooled our heels briefly in the ad hoc band room, and then Zappa came out to greet us, if that's the right word. He had a reputation, especially in those early days, for—shall we say—irascibility. Today we might say defensive, sarcastic, and on guard.

No sooner had we shaken hands, but Frank had moved on to something more important—tuning one of his many guitars, or whatever. Cowed by his apparent indifference (and my own near-veneration for this "psychedelic" pioneer), my mind began to back-pedal. *I had no opening question.*

We sat down at the mic. I tried to fight off feelings of insignificance as I read the sneer on his face as justifiable contempt for the craven media poseur that dared to waste his time. What could I ask him that would be unique and insightful, inspiring original thought? What hadn't he, who'd heard it all, not already been asked?

I'd been silent too long. Zappa and the promo guy were regarding me with concern. I took a deep breath (a form of silent prayer) and asked:

"Could you tell us whether the fact that you have incorporated influences from Edgar Varèse, free jazz, surrealism, and beat poetry meant that you think that rock 'n' roll is more than a commercial soporific, or should be?"

"What?! For a teenage radio station? Are you serious?"

"What I'm asking is whether it's *you* that's asking to be taken seriously."

A long silence as we stared at each other.

Then he smiled. Well . . . grinned.

And we were off on the first of what would turn out to be a series of eight interviews I'd be invited to conduct with this 20th Century master; the last one shortly before his tragic premature death.

On a much later occasion, in the heat of one of his endless legal battles, I sat down with Frank in a bungalow at the Beverly Hills Hotel. I'd just read an article in a Warner Bros. house organ asserting that Zappa's audience was really two audiences: a serious music-loving audience that came for his guitar solos, and a raunchy, comedy-prone audience that came for his brilliant satiric lyrics.

I set up the recorder and asked Frank whether he thought that was a fair statement.

About half an hour later he regained his composure, so exercised at what he considered not an artistic analysis at all, but the kind of facile marketing ploy of which record companies never tire.

"No, it's not right!" he erupted. "It's totally [expletive]!" He tried to restrain himself. "There's no division! My audience comes for both words and music. Stupid." And we went on from there.

A decent opening question, if I say so myself, but also a bingo question—a question that acts as a divining rod for great answers buried beneath the surface.

More about that later.

The other really horrible opening question I inflicted was, I'm embarrassed to report, served up to no less than one of the great jazz geniuses of all time, pianist/composer Bill Evans.

Evans had just changed record labels, signing with a huge corporate West Coast company that, in their wisdom, had consigned this immortal pianist—veteran of the Miles Davis Quintet, his own legendary trios (among other groups), and composer of "Waltz for Debbie," "Peace Piece," "Turn out the Stars," and other jazz classics—not to a proper jazz department (which they didn't have) but to a newly constituted "jazz and progressive" department, consisting of rockers, "fusion" players, . . . and the one and only Bill Evans.

My assignment, should I have chosen to accept, was to ask him questions (God save me) that would "help the rock audience relate to him." My heart sank at the proposed perfidy, but the opportunity to hang out with a bona fide jazz giant proved irresistible. I was given a table at all his Southern California gigs, and finally had to take my lickin'.

I presented myself at his hotel room, thinking, "Might as well get it over with," and for my opening question, I asked:

"What do you have to say to a rock audience?"

Evans looked at me as he might have at the sole of his shoe after noticing a bad smell. I held my breath.

"Nothing I can think of."

"Don't you think that since jazz and rock have their origins in the blues, there's a basis for common ground?"

"Not really."

Now I love all kinds of music: jazz, classical, Latin, blues, Hawaiian slack-key guitar, and, yes, rock 'n' roll. Until recently I'd passed for a rock disc jockey. I desperately wanted Evans to acknowledge some sort of connection to rock that would bring younger audiences, steeped in the Beatles, to his music. Relentless, I trudged forward.

"Is there anything about rock 'n' roll you find valuable?"

"No."

Silence.

"Useful?"

"No."

Longer silence.

"Helpful in making converts to your music?"

"I can't see how."

Stony silence.

At this point, sensing impending doom, I made a jump-shift. Leaving the mic on the table with him, I slipped out of my chair and took my place—where I should have been already—once again on the floor. Not only did this maneuver redress the cosmic balance, as it were, but it left me off-mic and the laconic Mr. Evans responsible for getting words onto tape. I could ask questions to direct his response, but he was well aware that my voice would be almost inaudible.

Used to playing solo, duets, or in a trio setting, Evans subtly shifted back to solo. Though I was now functioning at a level not much higher than page-turner, I managed to steer the conversation back to more congenial climes: Miles Davis, then and now, the future of jazz, his readings of Chopin, Debussy, Ravel, and Satie, and finally the new album. The record company's needs were satisfied, and I was ecstatic. But it took extreme measures to save myself from my own bad opener.

The Power Gush

In general it's basic good manners to open an interview on as positive a note as possible. I have always found some element of my subjects' lives and/or work to lead with. In the extremely rare case that I can't locate some praiseworthy aspect, I turn it down. What's the point?

Even if you are assigned a politician or lawyer to interview, my bet is that you can find some redeeming particle of value in her/his life or work to start off. You can always balance the big gush with the hard question, which we'll get to later.

The Follow-Up Question

In this section we return to the topic of LISTENING. Just as in music, listening is as important as actually playing. For example, the reason that the best classical musicians are drawn to chamber music (string quartets, etc.) is that the exposed nature of each part allows and, in fact, requires that each player listen closely to all the others, to hear the phrasing, the tempo, the dynamics, the blend of the instruments into a greater whole.

In jazz, listening is probably even more important because not only is it as exposed, but there is an "in-the-momentness" required of each player, demanding the instantaneous shifts and changes we call improvisation, the interaction of Preparation and Inspiration.

Please listen. From listening flows the right follow-up question.

1) Listen to the content of your subject's response to your opening question.

   ◆ Did he/she pause before answering? (If your opener was successful, your guest may need to do original thinking before framing an answer.)

   ◆ Was the response what you expected? If it was, is there a way you can tie the response to a question you've prepared, or one that occurs to you in the moment? The closer you listen, the more often a spontaneous follow-up question will arise like magic, effortlessly from your well-prepared brain. For example, ask yourself: Is there a character in your subject's book, play, or movie who you suspect may embody certain of subject's attitudes, ideas, or life experience? Play the hunch! E.g., "Is

Hamlet speaking for you, Mr. Shakespeare, when he says, 'The play's the thing'?"

♦ Did your subject's response confound your expectations? If so, how did it differ? Is there something in the divergence pattern that can be explained by something you've read about your subject? If the response is radically different, quickly locate the element that surprised you, fooled you, shocked you, and ask your guest to explain.

If you have the presence of mind to be able to formulate a succinct challenge to the part of the response that surprised you, do it. Your audience may have experienced the same dislocation, and is dying to hear the explanation. The simplest ploy is to ask for amplification. Anything from Mike Wallace's famous "Tell me," to "Really, that's the first time I've heard that. Let's hear more," to "Go on, Mr. Gibson, I'd really like to hear why you think George Bush is a Communist . . ."

2) Closely observe body language, voice tone, and other intuitive data.

♦ Be sensitive to body clues: breathing, voice, posture, and look. A relaxed person's breath is deep and steady. You can observe this by literally watching the chest rise and fall, or by listening to the voice: did it come rolling, calm, relaxed, and well-modulated from the diaphragm? Or piping, tense, tight, high from the upper chest? Was the voice full of life, happy to be there, or enervated, dull as dirt, and bored to the point of clicking on automatic pilot?

♦ What was on your subject's face as he or she responded to your opener? A smile? A wince? A grimace that says: Yuck! *that* question again? What about the eyes? Are they flashing and ready to engage, or dull, dead, bummed, and signaling the publicist to get the car? And what about the body language? Is your subject on the edge of the chair, loose and alert? Or, are your subject's hands crossed on the chest, rigid and detached?

Not all of these observations will—or should—take the form of conscious notations. More likely your subconscious will record it all, with the conscious mind freed to spot only the key emotional indicators.

Trust your gut. If you sense that your subject is not psychically engaged, take whatever steps necessary to wake up his or her slumbering *chi*. In any case, keep your own energy up—not manic or happy-talky, just relaxed, interested in your subject, and focused.

Interviewing is a profoundly human endeavor, a high-level communication of important ideas, opinions, feelings, and style that can be complex as it is often profound. So all the above need to be taken into account before:

Twin Troughs

Unless you wish to appear doltish, please avoid the following:

The infamous itinerary question: e.g., "So! Where do you play next?" "Ah, Pittsburgh! I love Pittsburgh!"

The deadly influences question: e.g., "So! Who influenced you as a young (musician, politician, sprinter, etc.)?"

An influences question always needs to contain evidence that you have studied the guest's life and work and can detect some of the influences yourself, e.g., "It seems that you've listened to the great Bob Marley as a young musician and maybe Marvin Gaye as well . . .?"

Nothing drives audiences to their remotes or car-stereo buttons faster than these beneath-the-bottom-of-the-barrel, epitome-of-routinism approaches.

The Big Silence

If you feel an answer is stingy, incomplete, or inadequate, try saying nothing, keeping the mic under your subject's nose, while looking intently at them as if you're too polite to interrupt. In most cases your guest will proceed to elaborate, giving you time to scan your mind for a suitable redirection in the extremely rare case that your subject simply clams up, looks away, or starts humming.

There's a (perhaps apocryphal) "big silence" story about Igor Stravinsky, arguably the greatest classical composer of the 20th Century, on the occasion of his first American radio interview.

The host for this widely ballyhooed interview on a prestigious New York classical station made the Maestro welcome, announced to his audience how proud he was to have Stravinsky on the show, then began the historic interview with his opener:

"Maestro Stravinsky, I've always thought of you as primarily a man of the theater—your famous ballets, extraordinary operas—most of your compositions seem to me to be essentially dramatic. Am I right?"

The great composer smiled, then sat and thought for a while, and finally nodded his head soundlessly in the affirmative. There was a silence, the dreaded dead air. Stravinsky was beaming. The host was not. Staring desperately at the composer, who was now turning his head from side to side, to share his smile with the small crowd of publicists, managers, and culturati in the small broadcast studio. Finally his gaze returned to the speechless host. But too much time had passed.

The host cleared his throat and asked another question. This time the Maestro reflected for a long moment, reached out to place his hand on the trouser leg of the host's sharkskin suit, and silently shook his head in a silent "no."

But there was only one Igor Stravinsky, and he died in 1971. So unless you find yourself in an interview with an equally magnificent cosmic joker, the big silence should not backfire. But, as always, be prepared. Plan B is always welcome.

The Hard Question

Sometimes your assignment is to ask the hard question, one that risks a hostile or defensive response at the least, and a precipitous termination of the interview (and nasty e-mails to your boss) at the most. It's the chance you take. Be prepared to pack up and go home.

Believe it or not, the hard question is actually easier in the news/ public affairs/political analysis interview than in the sports, personality, artistic/scholastic/scientific areas. For one thing, politicians, newsmakers, criminal lawyers, drug lords, NATO spokespeople, etc., are used to answering hard questions (or what sometimes pass for them). Unlike many a sports figure or celebrity, they won't cut and run as soon as the prearranged puff questions are replaced with honest interrogatives—they'll often answer them (it comes with the job), or else prevaricate, or pull a "nixon."

A *nixon* = "Let me say this about that." And then change the subject.

Seldom is the hard question the opener. Unless you are doing cutting-edge investigative or political interviews and constantly having to shoot from the hip whenever you can get one of your often-elusive subjects to hold still for your cameras or microphones, it just makes better psychological sense to give your subject a chance to relax before you blindside him or her.

In my experience, unless you're assigned not to come back without the toughie, it is wiser to let it ride until you've got everything else you wanted to get on film or tape already in the can. THEN reach back and slip it to 'em. That way if they bolt, you're covered.

In the Gore Vidal interview described earlier, in which I consciously and dramatically sat at his feet, I let him completely explicate his new book's thesis before asking the hard question. In the process he told wonderful stories about being stopped at the border and his censored "no politics" appearances on *The Tonight Show*.

The new book asserted that the U.S. had become a "National Security State" and that big media was a cornerstone of that state. It was a brilliant analysis (whether you agree with it or not), elegantly put forward in his juicy mid-Atlantic voice. When I had enough tape for weeks and weeks of shows, I asked what I thought was a fair question given his view of American society:

"How does a person of your background, with generations of Tidewater landownership and establishment political power, come to hold such radical views of American social structure?"

A pause. Gore Vidal fixed me with a magisterial glance.

I continued. "Could it have been your homosexuality that first gave you the outsider's perspective from which . . ."

"Americans!" he snorted dismissively.

I took a deep breath—held it—and kept the mic pointed at him. Looked expectant.

"Europeans would understand this. No. I reject the American notion of what you call 'homosexuality.' There is no 'homosexuals.' Only homosexual *acts*!"

"But . . ."

"What a travesty. The 'gay lifestyle.' Really! Tell me what *that* is."

Now, I'm a great respecter of personal privacy, even for an international celebrity such as Gore Vidal. Also, I'm nothing like a gay-basher, nor was I trying to "out" Vidal, who is long out of the closet, if he ever was in one. My question was not an attempt to exploit a "sizzle," nor to embarrass or distress my subject in any way. It was a question that—on the evidence—begged to be asked, one to which I thought I knew the answer, however aware of the chance I was taking. A hard question can end an interview.

The Bingo Question

Sometimes hard questions turn out to be bingo questions—a Zen arrow of an interrogatory thrust so well-launched that it strikes something in your subject that even he or she didn't know was there (or had forgotten), lying dormant in the depths, waiting only for your question to erupt. Ideally, interviews should be nothing but bingo questions. How many you elicit depends largely on:

- Preparation
- Opening Question
- Listening
- Experience
- Intuition

If you've:
1) done your homework;

2) achieved your goals with your opener;

3) concentrated totally on your subject's response; and

4) avoided his/her resistance patterns as you peeled away the layers of the onion, then follow your gut to . . .

. . . the BINGO QUESTION!

One of my earliest bingos came in a live interview I did with Country Joe MacDonald of the rock group Country Joe and the Fish. Joe was and is a bright, politically savvy, art-oriented (as opposed to commerce-oriented) band leader/writer/lead singer, who saw himself as an antiwar militant as well. Yet he turned out to be as affable a subject as you might wish for. He and the Fish had just played a major gig in town, and he was relaxed and ready for anything when he took a seat in my little On-Air booth.

Live interviews can be tricky, especially with volatile, rebellious, hippie rock stars with a penchant for profanity (we had no time-delay provision). But I was most concerned about coming off too crass and commercial, so I tried to keep the freeform conversation that ensued as elevated as possible.

It was going great; we talked about San Francisco in '67 ("The Summer of Love"), Paris in '68 (the students' and workers' strike), and serious stuff like that. Yet welling within me was a question that I had to ask, even though it might really piss him off. Finally, when the mutual *bonhomie* had reached a righteous level, out it popped:

"How do you deal with the fact that you have had only one hit? Does it bug you? What are your goals in regards to the pop charts?"

"Damn! Ya know just last week I was at a Doors concert up in Minneapolis. And they're a dynamite band, but I kept thinking, 'These kids aren't even listening. They're gettin' high, groping each other, and every once in a while lookin' up and screamin' at the stage: "Play 'Light My Fire,' man!"'

"'Cause that's the only tune the radio ever plays. Just like they only play our 'Fish Cheer/Feel Like I'm Fixin' To Die Rag.' So, like, do you give 'em the hit first and have most of 'em leave after they hear it, or do you save the hit for last and have 'em noddin' out before ya get to it?"

BINGO. Despite his art, politics, and international acclaim, Country Joe had to think about radio rotation, hit singles, pop charts, and distribution just like mortal men.

I've referred to the *first* of my two interviews with Leonard Bernstein, but it was during the second time I interviewed him, some five years later, when I asked him . . .

The Hard Question (actual transcript):

MP: The last time you and I talked, we discussed a thing that you were working on, from Thornton Wilder's *The Skin of Our Teeth*, that was—

LB: About five years ago . . . a sad subject, 'cause it all collapsed . . . in collaboration . . .

MP: The question I ask is that with your unquestioned powers for communication in so many different areas and your ability to write music that would be better than *Hair*, presumably . . . are you now interested in writing?

LB: I don't think it would be better if I tried to write rock music, for example. I don't think I could write a better . . . or even as good . . .

MP: You don't think so?

LB: Probably not. I've never tried.

MP: What is the music of *West Side Story?*

LB: It's not rock . . .

MP: What is it?

LB: It's pre- . . . I don't know what it is . . . it's the music of *West Side Story* . . . [*chuckles*] I can't pigeonhole that.

MP: Well, would you be interested in writing something that . . .

LB: Yes!

MP: Pretends toward . . . some kind of . . . the fashionable word is . . .

LB: Yes.

MP: Or post-fashionable word is "relevance," that kind of . . .

LB: Yes, that's what's been hanging me up these five years since we talked—that's one of the reasons *Skin of Our Teeth* didn't reach completion. And I've had two similar projects since then on which I've spent anywhere from six months to a year on each one. One of them was an enterprise involving Jerome Robbins, based on a little Brecht play called *The Exception and the Rule,* which is nothing if not "relevant" and could have been, I still think, the most exciting theater piece that Broadway has ever had . . . and it just didn't work out, after a year of very hard labor. And we parted; gave it up. The third was a film project, an all-musical film, which I was planning with Franco Zeffirelli on the life of St. Francis, and I spent six months on that one. And our ideas began to diverge more and more, and we saw after five months or so that it was not going to be possible to have any unanimity of feeling, so I had to give that up. And the result is that I have piles of music lying around of unfinished things and nowhere to use them because they're all so particularly specific, relevant to the given project. And in these cases the point I'm trying to make is that this "relevance" problem is the one that usually hangs us up as collaborators, and I haven't quite figured out why. It may have something to do with our generation, with an unwillingness to pander to youth by pretending we are, 'cause we aren't . . . the pre-Hiroshima generation and the kids are post-, and a great unwillingness on my part to take advantage of current trends, sort of get on a bandwagon, do pseudo-rock nonsense. In other words it's a matter of finding out exactly what I can do now. I would have known if I'd continued, if I'd continued after *West Side Story* and written the next show and the next and the next. I think by now . . .

[GRAND PAUSE . . . *The dozen or so members of the press, hangers-on, etc., drew breaths. Less than a gasp, it was nevertheless a collective intake audible to even the inattentive observer. The Maestro looked down at the table. The moment hung in the late spring air. Then he sighed. A deep sigh as if from an excavation. I held my breath.]*

. . . I would have found what I was looking for. But for better or for worse, I did accept the N.Y. Philharmonic at that point . . .

MP: [*light sarcasm*] I do recall that . . .

LB: That was '57; that was 13 years ago. Long time. And I was absolutely sure at that point that there were dozens of young kids around, composers, theater people who would leap in and take the next step after *West Side Story*, which pointed a direction, it seems to me, having broken ground that was fairly clear. But, instead, the country has happened to the Broadway musical scene, it's retrogressed, fearfully, it's gone back to *Mame*s and *Hello Dolly*s, which represent the infancy of, and the infantilism of, the American musical theater instead of having taken a step forward. There are a couple of exceptions to that: *Company* is one exception, by Steve Sondheim; *Fiddler on the Roof* made some attempts, but I don't think it's really first-class material.

MP: But there are other kinds of "relevance" without, as you say, pandering to a youth market. You don't have to write rock 'n' roll music . . .

LB: That isn't all I mean by relevance . . .

MP: Or take advantage of the trends and trendiness of writing for the market, you could certainly do other things—it seems—of course it's easy to say . . .

LB: I'd have to pick up the pieces from 1957 now.

BINGO again.

Or consider the interview with the late Judith Campbell Exner, beautiful party-girl friend to Frank Sinatra, the leadership of the Chicago mob, Bobby Kennedy, and JFK himself.

She told me that on weekends when Jackie was out of town, Judy would receive the usual call from then-President Kennedy. He'd send a limo for her, clear her through Secret Service Security and send her into a special presidential boudoir.

I was recording an interview with Judy the week her tell-all book came out, sitting on her patio overlooking Newport Harbor. She'd already given me juicy, then-scandalous stories about how the CIA had paid millions to mobsters Johnny Roselli and Sam "Momo"

Giancana to assassinate Fidel Castro by defoliating the Cuban president's celebrated beard, and the way the Rat Pack/mob/White House connection worked. Judy and I were dishing along famously, despite the brooding presence of her well-muscled, younger new husband, so I figured I'd go for it.

"How would you describe Jack Kennedy as a lover?" I asked her. "Did he know his way around a beautiful woman's body?"

"Are you kidding?" she laughed. "His idea of lovemaking was to stretch out on the bed, watch me as I undressed, then cop the identical plea every time I visited him in the White House: 'I've got a bad back, Judy. Would you mind just hopping on top and . . . ' Every time! The great lover."

Aaaaand . . . BINGO!

Just a few months ago I had the opportunity finally to meet André Watts, whose place is unique in music and in cultural history generally. A true war baby, his mother was Hungarian, his father an African-American G.I. A brilliant teenage piano virtuoso, the handsome young Watts had burst upon international consciousness endorsed by no less than Leonard Bernstein on one of his CBS *Young People's Concerts* telecasts.

In his dressing room we talked about "projection"; how, what, and why a performer sends *Hamlet*, *The Black Swan*, *Maximus*, or the *Emperor Concerto* down the line to audiences. How does a musician "project" Mozart? He gave me major insight. I was digging it immensely, feeling him absorbed in the thoughts that shaped his answer. Warming to his subject, he seemed to be opening personally to me, calling me "man."

Feeling comfortable—for the moment—I heard myself ask what might be the "out-the-door question":

"So, it's Black History Month, and I'd like to ask you for an essay: 'On Your Black-ness.'

You know you've asked a bingo question (for better or for worse) by the telltale silence that greets it. Tantric Emptiness, the Womb of All Phenomena. You remind yourself that there's a price for everything, and your subject has just become the cashier.

André Watts took a deep breath and laughed.

"Yeah, I'm the perfect one for that!"

And proceeded to give me 20 minutes on racism in America (and elsewhere); the differing influence of each parent; identity politics; racial-profiling by blacks and whites; and finally:

"I tell certain people: 'I'm half black and half white; got a problem with that?'"

(Bingo)

Over many years I've been fortunate to fashion questions sufficient to evoke a fair number of bingo responses, unanticipated responses that make perfect interview material. Some of the most memorable:

- Jazz singer Phoebe Snow's heartfelt soliloquy on growing up fat in New Jersey.
- Baseball Hall of Famer and stolen-base champion Lou Brock enunciating his base-bandit's credo: "Your approach to the game should be, 'How far can I go?' You must be able to seize the moment in a game and be able to live with the results."
- Conductor Sir Simon Rattle confessing that wily longtime L.A. Philharmonic Executive Director Ernest Fleishmann had been his father-figure.
- Elvis's bodyguard, Memphis Mafia member Sonny West, charging the still-living Presley with being "afraid to grow as an artist," citing as proof The King's refusal of Barbra Streisand's offer to play opposite her in *A Star Is Born*.
- Legendary jazz vocalist Rosemary Clooney confessing that her intellectual husband, actor/director José Ferrer, was so jealous of her close relationship with Bing Crosby that when the far more famous, but less-learned, Crosby came to dinner, Ferrer would try to establish dominance by goading the affable crooner into debate. To avoid these pointless ego-battles, Clooney's other best friend, frequent dinner guest Nat "King" Cole, would flee the table for the living room Steinway, where he would subtly serenade Rosie with her favorite tunes on the piano, as if to say "You and me, baby. And later for them—yeah."

A bingo answer is a rare and precious moment, when through your intuition and pertinacity you and your guest bring something new and valuable into being.

Summarizing

The ultimate fruit of listening is the developed ability of summarizing and restating your subject's views/life. A brilliant example of this mastery is regularly displayed by one of the best interviewers in public-affairs radio, Marc Cooper of nationally syndicated *Radio Nation*. Not only is he smart, well-informed, and a champion listener, but he is practiced in the art of quickly and cogently summarizing his guest's statements ("nutshelling") and restating them on-the-fly in ways that:

 + codify the interview up to that point
 + provoke further elaboration, and/or
 + redirect the interview to the next important point.

Here's what I heard Cooper do just this morning with two studio guests:

(Paraphrasing) "If I understand you correctly, Mr. X and Ms. Y, the issue comes down to American and, presumably, European multinationals providing nuclear bomb-building material to Iraq, while achieving plausible deniability through various loopholes backhandedly sanctioned by their individual governments. I know that as investigative reporters who have researched this situation extensively for a nonfiction film you're finishing called *Z Plus,* you must have some suggestions as to what we the people (who are the only ones left ignorant of this) can do to put an end to what appears to be a very dangerous practice."

Wow.

7

Types of Interviews

There are many different types of interviews, and every interview functions in more than one way. An official statement from the government becomes entertainment. A confessional moment with a superstar becomes big news. Your life as an interviewer is likely to include a wide range of intentions—sometimes artistic, sometimes commercial, hopefully both. Here's an overview of the interview landscape.

"Propaganda" Interviews

Propaganda interviews are interviews with any official, government representative, or politician or public figure that can put you in the position of parroting, or serving as a conduit for, the Official Version. Though these people usually operate through press conferences to disseminate their lines, they often do one-on-ones.

Your job in these cases is twofold:
- Allow them free rein to put forward their views; and
- Be sure that your follow-up questions provide your ultimate audience with a clear rebuttal, clarification, or exposure of contrary views. This should always be done impersonally, even if you yourself are an advocate for a diametrically opposite position.

Distance yourself with questions like:
- "Maureen Dowd in *The New York Times* called you a . . ."
- "Let me play devil's advocate on this one . . ."

This objectifying tactic will allow your audience to grasp the balance that you, as their representative, are providing so that they can make up their own minds.

Not all propaganda interviews come labeled as such. Historically, well-known media figures like Ronald Reagan (for GE and other corporate interests) and Charlton Heston (for the NRA and other corporate interests) initially emerged as spokespeople for points of view that they were not known to represent officially.

One of the most surprising examples in my personal experience was scientist, astronomer, author, and TV personality Dr. Carl Sagan. Dr. Sagan had become a national celebrity through his many appearances on *The Tonight Show*. I was so intrigued that I'd spent weeks wangling an interview with him on his only Los Angeles visit that year, at a conference called "California in the Space Age—An Era of Possibilities."

On the appointed day I found a seat in the main auditorium of the L.A. Museum of Science and Industry. The room was jammed with science-industry executives, aerospace notables, and a great number of military officers, in and out of uniform.

Dr. Sagan's speech was brilliant and warmly received. He touched on the wonders of space, known and unknown—the abundant educational possibilities alone—and strongly advocated an increased national devotion to further exploration. He concluded with a grand historical flourish, declaring that we stood in the same relationship to space as the 15th Century Europeans had to the New World: poised to capture its secrets. I looked around at the assembled brass, and had my doubts.

After his speech, Dr. Sagan was to meet me in a small exhibit room down the corridor from the main hall. I was finishing my set-up when he came in, greeting me with a manner both cordial and under pressure. I could tell he had to get back to the conference.

Nevertheless, I was so delighted to have this chance to talk with him that I asked endless questions about his new book, *The Dragons of Eden*, the "triune brain" theory, evolution, and finally, saving the hard (hopefully bingo) question for last: space. Here, Sagan, who'd been checking his watch every few minutes, seemed to relax and, in a foretaste of his persona on the brilliant PBS miniseries *Cosmos* (then still in post-production), began to wax rhapsodic. I sat enthralled as he took me with him out into deep space, floating through unexplored galaxies, past a seeming infinity of quasars, black holes, and supernovas.

Abruptly Dr. Sagan halted his narrative. Despite the fact that his people had promised me an hour, he was now preparing to leave with less than 30 minutes in the can. Since the interview was already a certain success, I couldn't resist the question that had been festering in my gut.

"One last question," I coaxed. (This always works in these cases because your subject can give you an answer of whatever brevity, assured of her/his choice of curtain line.)

"Shoot," he said.

"Well," I began, measuring the windmill, "in your speech you said that today we're in the same relationship to space as the European navigators had been to the New World—that we're on the brink of great discoveries, even colonizing space, as it were."

"Yes," he said. "It's a pretty straightforward analogy. They looked at us the way we look at the universe. Just a matter of expanded horizons."

I thought for a moment. What was a distinguished scholar doing in this morass of military-industrialites? Oh, well, here goes nothing: "Well, to me the analogy is flawed by failing to take into account the very different social and economic forces behind the two exploration waves you mention. In the 15th Century there was an emerging merchant and banking class whose search for financial gain—you know, tobacco, sugar, gold, cotton plantations, that sort of thing—fueled the expeditions to the Americas. Where is that class today?"

"What do you mean?"

"I mean who's going to pay for our adventures in space? Can we extract raw materials and bring them back profitably from space?"

"Not with existing technology."

"Also, we've just had an acute oil crisis; New York just went bankrupt; our cities are rusting; an epidemic of homelessness is abroad in the land . . ."

"We can do it," he said. "We just need to make it a national priority!"

Then I thought of the men in the main hall: NASA rubbing elbows with National Security Agency, Defense Department, Boeing, et al., and pressed STOP.

Was this all a pretext for handing the civilian agency NASA over to The Pentagon? They would certainly solve the problem of funding the further exploration of space. . . .

"Thank you so much, Dr. Sagan. It's been a pleasure."

But he was gone.

Propaganda interview? You tell me.

Promotional/Publicity Interviews

In a much smaller, more individual sense, the most common example of a propaganda interview often takes the form of a routine stop on a publicity tour. These media caravans are sponsored by publishers, record companies, movie studios, and various mega-publicists for anything from A-list supermodels to the World Trade Organization whenever it's time to get out there and push the product.

This is not to say you cannot do yourself proud. Some of my happiest interviewerly moments began life as a gleam in a PR person's eye. I tried to take these otherwise banal sell-a-thons as a challenge to go beyond the commodity aspect, to the heart and soul of whatever project I was becoming a complicitor in exploiting. In other words: if they give you lemons, make Key lime pie.

If Martin Scorsese has a new movie, don't turn down an interview with him for fear of pandering. Get in there, let him boffo the box office while you find some divinely inspired angle of inquiry that unlocks that great director's soul in a way that is unique and astounding. *Carpe diem*, for God's sake!

It's no secret that most of my interviews over the years had their genesis as a promotion for something. This remains true, certainly, in the arts, celebrity, sports star, and mainstream political world that constitute the interviewer's food chain. Perversely, I have always viewed publicity interviews as the Happy Hunting Grounds for bingo questions. The situation almost requires you dig for something novel and revealing.

"Live" In-Studio/On Location

We've already dealt with the special "performance" quality of live interviews. Nothing is as gratifying as working in real time. For one thing, being "live"—without safety net—usually takes your work up a level or two. For another, when it's over, it's really over: no editing or other post-production "sweetening" to do. Finito.

So the structure of the live interview is identical to the taped or filmed interview—only more so. For one thing, you've got to juggle all the other elements of live media, which can include (depending on the format) time, commercial breaks, identifying your guest/subject(s), and more.

True, the higher up the media tree you climb, the more sophisticated the set-up. You may have a producer handling guests, telephone callers, segment times, breaks, etc. This is an individual matter, specific to the type of show, format, medium, etc. Still, certain universal truths remain: your opener had better be absolutely riveting, your follow-up ready and true. As for your emotional state: you need to achieve that combination of relaxation and extreme attention-paying that keeps you in-the-moment, steady, but ready for anything.

If you're lucky enough to be doing this every day you will have already developed a rhythm, which should make all of this preparation routine and automatic. You may have at least a minimal staff to handle the research and even the actual questions. But if this is a first time, an occasional gig, or fill-in for you, bring your work shoes. Because in "live" work, if you fail, you fail big time—a failure that can cause severe career-death.

My favorite "live" interview (other than the Country Joe MacDonald on-air encounter) was not so much a product of preparation as of heads-upness and dumb luck. I was covering the Grammy Awards solo—a guy and his microphone—for the big Los Angeles classical station KFAC. My assignment: the relatively simple and straightforward job of writing and voicing periodic live reports on what "classical artists" were winning what awards, as the winners were announced.

Now, "classical artists" generally pay almost no attention to the Grammys, seeing them as having little or no relationship to artistic achievement. Their "so what" attitude, however, is not shared by their record companies, who naturally view the little statuettes as marketable commodities, and try to encourage the nominees on their talent rosters to attend the long and arduous ceremonies. Few if any comply.

An exception the night of my assignment was the pioneer African-American Metropolitan Opera goddess Leontyne Price, present to receive a Lifetime Achievement Award. Ms. Price was standing in a small group of handlers, Grammy officials, and friends, looking somewhat lost; out of her element. It was ten minutes till the studio came to me for my hourly "live-shot," but I had a better idea.

You must believe that I was motivated more by the urge to save this magnificent diva, who had enriched the world so much with the gift of her artistry, from the media-squalor than with scoring a minor broadcast coup. I was no paparazzo, after all, nor was it my assignment to track down embarrassed honorees and hector them with "How does it feel to win a Grammy . . . ?" questions. No, I was, as much as anything, impelled to pay back some of the joy she'd brought me over the years with her great soprano voice.

I approached the divine Ms. Price, introduced myself, somehow convinced her I was not just the usual clinker journalist, and when the studio called with my "ready" cue, I told the producer what was up. He had the sense to blow out some commercials to give me room for a solid ten-minute mini-tribute, complete with music we scrambled to insert on the fly. Today this would be no big deal—except in classical music radio, where everything is a little slower than elsewhere—but it was a thrill for me at the time. And a good example of what can be done live.

Another thrill was an all-night session with the awesomely intellectual French composer/conductor/modern-music theorist Pierre Boulez. M. Boulez was in Cleveland studying conducting under George Szell, one of an assistant conductor corps that included Robert Shaw, James Levine, and Louis Lane among others. I got a message that Boulez had agreed to do an on-air fundraiser for the orchestra on the sole condition that he be provided a sufficiency of Haig & Haig "Pinch." Not wishing to offend the Maestro (who 20 years later would return to record with the same Cleveland Orchestra an unbelievably brilliant series of French music for Deutsche Grammophon) or lose the inter-view op, needless to say, I hopped on the scotch.

Initially I was in agony. My meager knowledge of rigorous avant-garde music was certain to be publicly revealed and reviled. I would be held up to ridicule for even daring to appear with such an icon. True, I knew some of Boulez's difficult modern compositions (disso-nant pointillism, really)—but certainly not well enough to dissect it meaningfully on-air live for five or six hours. But I need hardly have worried; in this case, I was saved by the bottle. As the hours passed, and the amber liquid flowed, we both loosened up: me from my fear of exposure, and him from whatever complexities the brilliant French Maestro's brain might have otherwise imposed.

Maybe that's why he asked for the bottle.

Multiple Subjects (Guests)

There is only one rule in multiple-subject interviews: Give it your best shot. Because of the fickle nature of group dynamics, every encounter with more than one guest is potentially a disaster—and more often brilliant. Decide in advance whether you want to spell out ground rules to the guests (practically imperative in live formats) or, like the Zen archer, launch your microphone/minicam into the maelstrom of, for example, Nine Inch Nails, and take your chances. In time you will find some combination of planning and improvisation that will allow you to keep order while encouraging maximum spontaneity from your subjects.

In radio you run the risk, whenever you turn a group loose live, of forcing your audience to guess who's talking when. So you must be ready to jump in and ID the guests as their identities begin to blur and their conversation becomes a cacophony of high-spirited but undifferentiated verbalization. On the other hand, if you're taping, you can always insert IDs as necessary. Always bear in mind that when individuals step on each others' statements, they become more difficult to edit cleanly.

In TV the job is somewhat simplified by never having to stop the flow of interview to remind the audience that "our guests today are . . ."—data that can be handled by superimposed graphics. In radio it's an absolute necessity. You must say: "We're talking with historian Ann Eccles, author of a new book on Janis Joplin; as well as Kobe Bryant of the Los Angeles Lakers, and . . ." and you must say it often, because of the nature of the medium. People tune in to radio every second, and deserve to know what or whom they're hearing. You must also ID the station, the name of the show, and your name, as well as giving the time, and forward-promoting what's next: "Coming up after the break, we'll be talking to Giorgio Armani about his new record label, Mike Judge about his new theme park, and . . ."

Multiple guests can turn your interview into a tag-team match, and you into a Socratic referee, especially if you all know you're broadcasting live, and can't stop tape and re-shoot after the smoke clears. This happens to good effect most often in political and public affairs shows, where truth goes whirling about the room, from guest to guest, "and where she stops, nobody knows."

Some of the most virtuoso multiple-guest interviews of recent years were turned in by numerous CNN hosts during the 9/11 crisis. These superb media professionals—Joie Chen, Bernard Shaw, and their colleagues—handled simultaneous multiple interviews, often through remote feeds, usually in different cities, both live coverage and taped.

Brilliant.

Exemplary.

They are seasoned, experienced pros who rise to the challenge of the pressurized moment. Yes, they have enormous staffs, research assistants galore, cue cards, stage managers, directors, and producers. Still, when you come down to it, it's a live performance, and the onus lies on the interviewer to be on and smooth.

Among my own personal most-memorable multiple-guest interviews were:

- The Roches (Maggie, Terre, and Suzzy): the pop trio of articulate sisters who wrote and sang their way into America's hearts in the late '70s, and whose infectious mutual one-upping made for a great series of interviews, as they routinely corrected each other, stepped on each others' lines, sang examples of their music in three-part harmony, and generally liquefied the microphone with their charm.

- The Labeque Sisters (Katia and Marielle): The extraordinary French duo-piano sisters have achieved, from childhood, such an interwoven, braiding rapport that the interview seemed almost an analog of one of their performances, intertwined and mutually responsive.

- The Casadesus family (Robert, Gaby, et Jean): The famous dynasty of French piano masters assembled in Cleveland for the Mozart three-piano Concerto, K. 242. Since proper pronunciation is the hallmark/bane of classical music announcing (which I was doing at the time), and the correct way to say their name was hotly disputed among announcers, I asked that each individually give the audience his or her pronunciation of their famously disputed surname.

The father, Robert, said: "Casa de Soose," explaining that it was originally a Spanish name, "Casa de Jesus" (house of Jesus) and, although he was born French, he had inherited his ancestors' inflection; the mother, Gaby, said it the way most Americans tried to say it: "Ca-*sa*-duh-soo"; but the very, very Parisian son, Jean, gave us: "Casad-sihh" (approximately). So, since there was no agreement among the family of artists themselves, it appeared that I'd performed a great public service; from that day forward the rest of us could stop worrying about it.

Dangers/Caveats

You may have already gleaned that there are more hazardous occupations than conducting interviews for a living, or even a school assignment or rewarding pastime. Life and limb are seldom threatened, and with the exception of exhausted patience or a bruised self-concept, interviewing presents few dangers. There are, however, a few caveats.

Routinism

Once you've landed a position as host, reporter, or regular correspondent, and are doing interviews on a regular basis, two things happen, only one of them good:

Upside
You tend to develop a rhythm that, like a hitting streak, can raise your confidence to higher and higher functioning levels, thereby reducing stress, increasing relaxation, and the concomitant powers of concentration.

Downside
Although a "beat" does not need to lead to routinism, once you've established a regular pattern, you may find that the cookie-cutter beckons. Every interview is, and should appear, unique, even if the guest is a repeat! Professionalism need not entail dullness. "Regular" need not translate as "boring." Mix it up. Stay fresh, open to whatever comes.

As mentioned earlier, I was privileged to be invited to conduct a total of eight interviews with composer/guitarist/satirist Frank Zappa between 1972 and his death in 1993. Usually these sessions would consume at least an hour and a kaleidoscopic range of topics. For one thing, the fact that these interviews were often years apart was almost a guarantee of freshness.

Things change, especially in the life of a dynamic creative/performing artist. Nevertheless, these were never simply news updates, reporting, for example, Zappa's career-long legal hassles with various record companies, managers, etc. Because of his depth of knowledge, experience, passion, and interests, there was always the opportunity to relate the present to some key element in his life or work. Maybe since I had established a tiny shred of believability with him, I was allowed to range over slightly broader terrain than the average visiting tape-monger: his adolescent R&B fanaticism, his father's playing "strolling crooner" guitar, family relations, the serious (modern classical) and jazz sides of his work, as well as the roots of some of his sharper social satire, from "Concentration Moon" to "Valley Girl" and beyond.

I emerged from these Zappa sessions with a greater understanding of him, the world, and even myself. I hope Frank felt something like the same thing.

The obvious point is: if you're thinking, "Been there; done that" about an upcoming interview, you're asleep at the cosmic switch. Go take a walk in the woods; do some yoga. Whatever. Your spirit needs refreshing. Routinism is another form of failure to prepare, in this case—yourself! Your guests and your audience deserve better than "another day, another tape session" treatment. This is not professionalism; and if you persist in this ho-hum attitude, your boss will take steps to remind you of that fact by replacing you with someone who cares.

We'll Meet Again

My mother used to say: "It's like kissin'; it depends on who!"

Interviews are like that: some of them you wish would go on forever; others you can't wait to end. So it is with the encore visit, or return encounter, a second, or third, or, in the case of Frank Zappa, eighth, interview with the same person.

My five interviews with Maestro George Szell had the virtue of ritual: every year as the Cleveland Orchestra Syndication Concerts, a regular season-opening visit with Szell was scheduled to kick-off the new broadcast year. In time these yearly interviews developed a cumulative ongoing, self-referential quality and became an annual fixture to which I looked forward with relish. My relationship with Dr. Szell grew from tolerant to avuncular to—I would like to think—something more, over the years.

These were rare, privileged situations. In general, if you barely stayed awake during your first interview with Mr. Blockbuster Director, it's doubtful you'll get a second chance, much less look forward to it. But it could happen—and the next time could surprise you.

BUT: what if you had to interview the same subject two days in a row? What if your first day's tape turned out to be flawed and unbroadcastable, and you had to—in essence—repeat the very same interview? What if the subject was one of the most honored of all Hollywood film composers, as well as a concert composer esteemed enough that Heifetz premiered his Violin Concerto? I was hosting *Martin Perlich Interviews* for The Grey Lady of L.A. classical stations, KFAC. My producer got a call from one of the children of the great Hungarian-American composer Miklos Rozsa, thee-time Oscar winner (among 13 nominations) for *Spellbound* (1945), *A Double Life* (1948), and *Ben-Hur* (1959).

Their father was in ill health and next week was his 82nd birthday; would we be interested in an interview while there was still time? We all agreed: it would make a great birthday present.

We drove to his home in the Hollywood Hills. The old man was brought down in a wheelchair, greeted us with a gravelly voice, and proceeded to regale us with stories of the Old Hollywood: Marlene Dietrich, Alfred Hitchcock—all that. A treasure trove of anecdotes, lessons, and pure narrative pleasure. This was the tape that proved useless. We called, my producer apologized: could we come back? Yes, yes, tomorrow would be fine.

So we went back. I still had my notes from the previous day, but was made incredibly uncomfortable, as I sat facing this Hollywood legend, by the presence of my tail between my legs. It was awful: embarrassment, loss of face, and the ineluctable necessity of asking questions that could only elicit foregone conclusions. I wanted those great stories from yesterday, and since Maestro Rozsa had health-shortened endurance, we didn't dare aim for more. So we settled, and I was in the position of acting surprised and attentive to what were for me old stories.

With a younger, healthier man I could have branched out, inter-larded the old questions with new. But in this case, given our culpability and the element of time, we played it safe, but it was excruciating: I felt like the William Hurt character in *Broadcast News*. But—and this is the point—the resulting shows were wonderful. And they aired during his birthday week.

I've already mentioned the eight sessions with Zappa, five with George Szell, two each with Leonard Bernstein, Martin Mull, and

Pierre Boulez, among others more and less notable. There are a few more two-timer anecdotes, and some lessons to learn from them.

Perhaps the most dramatic was one of the world's truly beautiful people, cellist and classical star-of-stars, Yo-Yo Ma, with whom I did two completely different interviews, one year apart. In the late '80s he had yet to achieve superstardom, but people who knew, knew he soon would—he was that good. And the way he looked when he played! A perfect definition of Out There. Yet I had interviewed him once previously at Dorothy Chandler Pavilion, and found him stiff and a trifle disengaged. But when I witnessed his onstage rapture as he soloed with the Los Angeles Chamber Orchestra, I decided to request another shot.

This time it was in his hotel. This time he welcomed me warmly. This time he sat in the very center of his slept-in bed and was so approachable that we ended up talking about his consciousness of his own subconscious when he played. I've heard both tapes recently and they sound like different people.

One of the great pleasures of doing interviews for 40 years (on and off) is the scope, the sense of personal and cultural history it has provided. Beside Zappa, Bernstein, and Szell, my life was enriched by at least tutorials with: André Previn, Taj Mahal, Anne-Sophie Mutter, Jackson Browne, Philip Glass, Martin Scorsese, Warren Zevon, Stephen Reich, Itzhak Perlman, Iona Brown, Randy Newman, Pandit Ravi Shankar, Robbie Robertson, and John Adams, among hundreds of others, but two glimpses (remember the French *entrevue—to see partially* or *to have a glimpse).*

And, thankfully, a pair with the great Isaac Stern, violinist extraordinaire, star of the acclaimed film *From Mozart to Mao*, and respected cultural ambassador. The two interviews were mid '60s at Severance Hall and late '80s in Beverly Hills. In 1965 he had been a dynamic young-middleaging virtuoso soloist and chamber player second to few, if any. By 1989 he had gained such a depth of understanding of things musical that I felt compelled to launch this unusually "philosophical" line of inquiry:

"What does music 'do'; I wouldn't ask this of many people, but I'm asking you."

"Imagine a day without sunshine," said Isaac Stern.

Another one of the past century's greatest violinists, Itzhak Perlman, was barely out of *wunderkindergarten* when I met and interviewed him on his first American tour, a brilliant young virtuoso arrived from Israel in a wheelchair. I was in my mid-twenties and don't recall much of what he said, but twenty years later when he came to KFAC to tape a pre-philharmonic interview, something had changed. Gone the tentative quality of the youthful immigrant; gone the hesitation in response to personal questions. So at home was the smiling Mr. Perlman that *he* relaxed *me*—to the point that I was able to lead him into uncharted territory for me: his own disability and his campaign to help the disabled.

We had both grown. Not that the first interview was a prerequisite, without which the second would have been poorer. But that the interview process is so endless, so involving, and so enriching, that with the right person it can be a constant and recurring lesson in lifelong learning. You see people age, change, grow, and become wiser . . . or not.

Another career-long repeater was Judy Collins, one of the very best of the folkie singer/songwriters. Though she sang more songs than she wrote, she has gone on to write op-ed articles for *The New York Times* as well as at least one best-selling novel. (Full disclosure: Judy became a friend, stayed at our house in Cleveland, was godmother to our oldest boy, and later asked me to be her manager.)

But at the time of the very first interview I hardly knew her; she was giving the first "folk concert" at Severance Hall, home of the Cleveland Orchestra, and there was a crowd of hippier-than-thou kibitzers in the green room as we taped. It didn't go brilliantly (I was light on the right questions to ask), but it wasn't a total loss.

I'd gone to hear her at subterranean La Cave and "fell in love" with her (the idea of Judy Collins, really, her music) and her famous blue eyes. In my living room her singing turned me on to "a Canadian writer named Joni Mitchell," "this guy in L.A. named Randy Newman," "the genius poet and novelist Leonard Cohen," and lots of unknown Dylan. Pretty soon I knew her whole repertoire.

Ten years of career-following later, I brought her to *The Midnight Special*, where, for her "Salute" interview she graciously narrated her entire life in music (with lavish song examples). At the end of taping, Director Stan Harris literally threw himself at her feet.

My final interview came for a radio-documentary I did for her record label, where she told of her blind DJ father, her affair with Stephen Stills, and much more. Knowing Judy Collins was one of the most lavish bounties of the interview life. Yet I never counted myself her peer, but rather enhanced my life with her art.

"Words and Music" (Tell & Show)

Since my primary area of interest was initially music, I found myself, early and often, with guests willing to play or sing as part of their appearance on my various shows.

Of course, if as an interviewer you're primarily involved with cooking, or poetry, say, or extreme sports, these tell & show shows will necessarily be different, but contain many of the same fundamentals.

In any case, there are two basic approaches:

1) Live in-studio (live, or live-to-tape)

A live show & tell is a live show & tell, whatever the guest's specialty. Your job is to keep things moving, elevating, and—beyond all else—worthy of your audience's attention, i.e., entertaining. With a musical guest your role is:

a) Part live concert announcer ("that was Bob Dylan, live in-studio here at WKRP, with 'Ballad of a Thin Man'");

b) Part disc jockey, keeping a mix of great music coming from your guest performer(s) ("Jimi, do you still do 'Foxy Lady'?"); and

c) Part interviewer, asking the questions that an intelligent TV or radio audience would or should want your guest to answer ("Mr. O'Dette, how on earth did you choose an instrument as arcane as the lute?").

Like most of the "rules" of interviewing in this slender volume, I learned these live show & tell techniques the hard way: *by doing it wrong.*

In the mid '60s I was doing an "eclectic" show, *The Perlich Project,* and had discovered a new LP by a West Coast folk group called The Stone Poneys. I dunno, I just liked their sound and was playing it a lot when their label called and asked if I would have them on live. Now, I had never done a live music presentation on my show, but figured, why not? Luckily I had an engineer who could solve the miking problems for three people playing and singing live in-studio, while I blissfully stumbled through my very first show & tell. No major mistakes, except I didn't recognize the name of, nor direct a fair share of questions to, the pretty "girl singer" whose name turned out to be Linda Ronstadt.

In time I would host many musical acts of the time, from Arlo Guthrie, reprising "Alice's Restaurant" from Newport, to one of the biggest (eight musicians) bands of the '70s, the original Blood, Sweat & Tears. But since I was on my own recognizance, the biggest lesson I learned was to trust myself as an audience member—what did *I* want to hear? Was I providing the right questions, music requests, etc., from my guests? If I liked it, I figured, why wouldn't the *rest of the audience?*

Documentary Form (Tape or Film)

Though I do occasionally present live music on my KCSN show (recently hosting a spellbinding live hour with Paul O'Dette, the world's greatest lutenist), I've had far more experience with "documentary."

Segments of pure talk and pure performance may be blended in post-production to produce a satisfying portrait of the musical artist, demonstrating by example how she/he composes, practices, plays, sings, or all of the above. Here, don't be afraid of using all the time-honored documentary techniques: voice-over; historic film/tape/stills; interviews with critics, industry observers, friends of the artist, family members, etc.

Preparation for these shows is absolutely paramount, especially in film and TV, where your every expression is under the spotlight, and every second is expensive:

Start with a show rundown: what music (hits, major contributions, etc.) to select to represent the subject. Study the music: know the lyrics of all songs, their meaning, importance, inspiration. If it's someone with hits (like Judy Collins, who was hot at the time we made the audio documentary "Hard Times for Lovers"), know the dates, etc., of the tunes, who else recorded them, chart history, and, most important, their authors. It will do no good to ask her a would-be insightful question about a song lyric, "Is 'Suzanne' autobiographical?" if it was written by someone else (Leonard Cohen).

Technically, documentary form has a few caveats: although you are interviewing your subject, the finished product will more often look as if the subject is talking directly to the camera, or conducting an internal monologue. This is, of course, your director's call, but be careful not to step on the audio; i.e., let your subject begin and end sentences *in the clear*, without your voice saying "uh-huh," or whatever. Ask any editor why. In film/video the director may want you in some shots; this too is her/his call. But for audio, when you may be your own director, what I have usually done is simply not mic myself. This has the additional advantage of acknowledging that the subject is on her/his own, and you can play "actor's director."

On *The Midnight Special*, our very popular documentary section, "Salute," was a weekly series of mid-career retrospectives of pop-toppers: from Aretha Franklin to Willie Nelson to Johnny Mathis to Ray Charles to you-name-it, we took the greatest stars of the period through quasi-biographical on-camera narrations. Basically they were "and-then-I-wrotes" writ large, with stills, concert footage, and whatever else we could get their "people" to find us, added in NBC editing bays. Worked pretty well, but it goes without saying that there were few bingo questions, and no hard questions were allowed.

For *Singer/Songwriter* I was able to ask some good questions, though only Randy Newman chose to answer them.

I did direct a pretty decent documentary-like video piece (in one cut, an "electronic press kit") on the great bluesman Taj Mahal, with whom I'd worked in the past, and whose repertoire I knew and loved. I shot him in studio at the piano, on the Sunset Strip in front of the *Whiskey a Go Go*, where he'd played with Ry Cooder when he first came to L.A. in the mid '60s, and on the Santa Monica Pier, singing his famous "Fishing Blues," playing guitar and strolling past a line of old guys fishing off the pier. Because of my "cred" with Taj, it was all pretty much unrehearsed, but was an easy edit. Despite my recommendations of interviewerly anonymity, I found it advantageous to stage an on-camera one-on-one interview with me actually questioning Taj about the old days. Bentleys, Bimmers, and buses whizzed by us as he apostrophized the Whiskey, then and now.

For radio it's sooooo much easier. For one thing I got a lot of practice. In the late '70s I hosted and produced a syndicated weekly hour called "Rock Around the World"—a rockumentary with lots of music, for which off-mic interviews were *de rigueur*.

Patti Smith, Tom Petty, Warren Zevon, Kenny Loggins, Carla Bonoff, Al Di Meola, Stanley Clarke, and many more simply popped up to intro, comment on, and contextualize their best tunes, while their records played under, through, and around them.

I also did a series of fairly spiffy interview/audio-mentaries on brilliant jazz/classical/minimalist musicians, including Philip Glass (on the making of the film *Koyaanisqatsi*), Steve Reich (on the occasion of the release of his masterpiece "Music for 18 Musicians"), and Pat Metheny.

But the most enlightening of these was "The Last Waltz" with Robbie Robertson, of The Band.

I'd been meeting with Robbie to develop a one-of-a-kind *Midnight Special* show for them and all the people who influenced them (Muddy Waters, Ronnie Hawkins, Dylan, Joni Mitchell, Neil Young, and others) to come on and jam. Just a darkened soundstage with no show logo, no (regular host) Helen Reddy, no (pitchman/Shakespearean fool) Wolfman Jack. Just too cool.

Next thing I knew they were doing something similar on Thanksgiving Day in San Francisco—as a feature film to be directed by Martin Scorsese, and to be called *The Last Waltz*. I got backstage passes for my trouble, and a lovely Thanksgiving dinner, which they served for the entire audience as the San Francisco Symphony played Strauss for dancing. Later when I interviewed Robbie for a radio documentary for Warner Bros. to promote the release of their *Last Waltz* three-LP "live" set, it was like I knew the understated leader of one of the era's pivotal rock bands (at least as well as many at a similarly distant remove).

People liked the hour radio special my company produced from the interview. I really liked Robbie Robertson and was delighted when his producer asked me to do a similar radio special on Robbie's feature-film acting debut, *Carney*, with Gary Busey and Jodie Foster, for which he'd also written original music.

Confusing Life and Art

A more dangerous blunder (and at the same time more enticing) is making the mistake of thinking you are on the level of your subject. In an era when media stars like Tom Brokaw, Peter Jennings, Barbara Walters, Dan Rather, Cokie Roberts, et al., are well-enough paid to be able to share neighborhoods, country clubs, and private schools with their guests, one may be excused for developing this delusion.

For the Superstar Anchors this constitutes a clear (if seamlessly stonewalled) conflict of interest; for you and me it is merely audience-alienating hubris.

In all the years I have done interviews, I have never (with the two key exceptions described below) confused myself with my subject. There may be a sense of collaboration in the taping or broadcast session, a sense of warm, coming together to create something new and special, of momentary intimacy, even. But when the interview ends, so does the association. As much as you might have wanted to think of yourself as intrinsically equivalent to Tom Hanks, Mark McGwire, or the Dalai Lama, common sense should assure you that, world-historically, this is not quite the case. They are not interviewing you, after all.

Au contraire.

In fact there is an obvious social danger in creating and maintaining celebrity newspeople. CBS superstar anchor Dan Rather confesses in his book, *Deadlines and Datelines*, that he did interviews which he openly refers to as "beat-sweeteners"—puff-pieces intended to paint unduly rosy TV portraits of influential people, people who could (and did) advance his career. My advice is to keep your distance. You'll sleep better, even if you live less lavishly.

This means avoiding open or obvious partisanship (pro or con), even when the issue is one you endorse or feel strongly about. Whatever you do off-camera, or mic, in the interest of your credibility, remember:

Enthusiasm does not entail professional advocacy. In other words, be fair or be subtle.

FULL DISCLOSURE: I have not always been "balanced," "professional," "distanced," "media-cool," or "fair." In the wake of the JFK assassination and the Warren Report discrepancies, I woke up sociopolitically. There was a period (1967-1977) when my belief in social justice began to lend my interviewing more of a sense of advocacy than today's journalism schools might permit.

It all started innocently enough with Ralph Nader, whose 1966 book *Unsafe at any Speed* attacked not only my father's car, the Chevrolet Corvair, but the cynical corporate malfeasance that buried evidence of the car's murderous steering deficiencies.

My interview with the future presidential candidate was an eye-opener: first of all, I was able to hang out with him backstage before a public lecture, get his recommendation for a car that *was* safe enough to trust my newborn baby in. Both informally and onstage it was impossible to miss his terrible sincerity. I was forcefully awakened to the reality: people needed to hear what he had to say (and not just about the Corvair)! And even I could help save lives; get the message out! Corporations needed strict oversight; their too narrow a focus on profit puts Americans at risk! Something seemed to be calling me.

My next adventure in this new Immersion Journalism was a mild one: a fancy hotel restaurant interview with the semi-official Artist Laureate of the psychedelic age, Peter Max. I approached the lunch meeting in the spirit of Max's joyful, carefree painting, with love in my heart. But I had a hidden agenda: his Warhol-like embrace of commercialism. Having purchased one of his sprightly but almost prohibitively expensive ties, I wore it to meet him, the large price tag clipped provocatively to the front of the cravat.

As it turned out this was just the Zen jape to dispense with all formalities. A wonderful, funny interview with a surprise ending: an act of instant creation. I'd been offered a free trip to take my growing family to India to explore spiritual practice. At the same time I was waiting for an answer from Leonard Bernstein on a project he had proposed. Either way, a long journey seemed to be staring us in the face. Which one? That was my bingo question for Peter Max. He responded by opening a clean linen napkin, whipping out a black marker.

"Should you go to India?"

And quickly produced the lovely Lady, Boat, and Mountain drawing that hangs in my bathroom.

Despite my increasingly activist thrust there were times during this period when I *was* striving to reach a broader audience by presenting a more "balanced" view. In these instances, I employed a strategy you might try in these far more corporate times, when you feel strongly about, say environmental, racial-profiling, spousal abuse, or other important issues: the simple Devil's Advocacy Ploy. Take yourself out of the picture by booking guests who put forward a view you may share, and asking them the questions a reasonable audience member would ask, given the opportunity. If they can't answer the questions honestly and to your satisfaction, maybe you ought to reconsider your position, but more importantly, you have done your job responsibly.

Because my audience was fundamentally opposed to the war in Vietnam, I was happy to schedule an interview with Ron Kovic on my interview show, *Electric Tongue*. And because of his fame a broader listenership was expected. So with a chance of winning hearts and minds (as we all thought we were doing) I wanted to be extra careful in my presentation.

A veteran of the Vietnam War, Kovic had considered it his duty to serve his country. For his patriotism he was rewarded with a bullet in his spine, paralyzed from the chest down. Later to become a national Hero of Conscience (in part through Oliver Stone's acclaimed film version of Kovic's autobiography, *Born on the Fourth of July*, in which he was played by Tom Cruise), Kovic was, when I sat down with him in 1971, struggling to bear moral witness to the cruelty and immorality of war.

Now, in the simplest sense, I intended my interview with Kovic to play as antiwar propaganda, pure and simple. Today we'd call that an unbalanced journalistic approach. In those days ethical subtleties of this kind often fell by the wayside, but I felt the greater good would be served by playing it straight. So rather than expose myself as a peace advocate, I played straight interviewer, putting to Ron all the objections that pro-war Americans had already voiced. It was certainly clarifying to hear Ron Kovic answer these objections. Through this sort of presentation, I dared to hope, the end of the tragic war would be seen as a moral imperative.

He was electrifying: leaning into the mic from his wheelchair, telling war stories, but just as moving as his own personal injuries were the radical changes his previously gung-ho mindset had undergone. In a series of incidents subsequently given short shrift in the movie, Kovic described his disenchantment with his government's lies and the real goals of a war in which he and his fellow soldiers had given so much. Moving stuff.

Going Native or Just Going With the Flow?

I was slipping into complicity. Never trained as a journalist (or anything else, for that matter), I was beginning to use my interviews as a way of speaking out against the war, racism, corporate domination, etc. Foreign correspondents have described what was happening to me as "going native." From my new position as Public Service Director of a "progressive" rock station, WMMS in Cleveland, this provided some unique cultural moments:

An interview with the brilliant San Francisco poet Lawrence Ferlinghetti, during which my tape recorder and I deserted objectivity completely, kneeling with him on the floor of his moderate-priced motel in anti-war prayers, ending with a broadcast-quality "Coca-Cola Mantra." Amen.

A not-entirely sober broadcast with Firesign Theatre founding member Peter Bergman (full disclosure: Peter briefly dated my sister) in which we jammed on riffs from the amazing satirical sketch group's last album: *Rrrr-ocka-feller; Rrrr-ocka-feller; Nix-on; Nix-on*. Listeners to WMMS in Cleveland called the radio station: "Do you know your mics are open?"

I covered antiwar demos at The Pentagon, and the Kent State Memorial; interviewed Farm Workers Union organizers and VVAW (Vietnam Veterans Against the War) members. But the most involved I became with social movements was a trip to Detroit to cover *The Winter Soldier Investigation* with Jane Fonda and Donald Sutherland. I had interviewed the future Ms. Ted Turner before the weekend hearings, which I attended at her invitation, and whose startling revelations stirred deep pacifist notes within. War was not healthy, I concluded.

So, though the rule of thumb is: you are friendly with your subjects, not their friend, I can recount two examples of my crossing the line into real-life personal adventures with my guests, one hair-raising and ultimately silly; the other a once-in-a-life time opportunity that ended in heartbreak.

The "hair-raising but silly" story concerns an L.A. hippie paper at the height of the antiwar movement. The paper, which featured radical politics, naked women, and other (only slightly more savory) examples of counter-cultural effusions, had been banned by Orange County authorities. I was hosting *Electric Tongue*—the two-hour interview show I did on the L.A. "underground" rock station KMET. Seeing the show (with a grandiosity that befitted the period) as "a voice of the oppressed, and beacon of democracy," I felt honor-bound to invite the editors of the suppressed journal on my show.

At the taping I expressed solidarity with the editors, then took them to task for featuring only *women's* naked bodies in their paper. Attempting to turn proto-political correctness on its head, I more or less accused them of sexism.

"Why are there no naked *men*?" I asked.

At first they claimed they'd tried to recruit nude male models, but had no takers.

I laughed this to scorn, "In Hollywood? Are you kidding?"

One of the editors, an attractive woman, took this opportunity to unfold a ravishing smile, and slyly parry:

"Of course, we'd be delighted if *you'd* like to volunteer. . . ."

The second interview I did with Leonard Bernstein led to a proposed professional association with the Maestro that literally changed my life.

The morning after the interview I was sitting around in my nightshirt when the phone rang. It was the manager of The Cleveland Orchestra:

"Lenny wants to see you."

"Lenny who?"

I actually did say this before considering the context. He straightened me out and continued.

"He's staying down in a motel, near Blossom Music Center, and wants to hear from you. Give him a call."

I jumped in the car and an hour later Leonard Bernstein was filling me in:

"My contract with CBS is up for renewal in September," he was saying, "and this new person, this Davis, this lawyer, is not necessarily a friend of our music."

Clive Davis (now one of the sainted heads of the record industry) had just taken over the reins as president of Columbia Records from Lenny's old personal friend, Goddard Lieberson, the previous year.

"He's just discovered rock 'n' roll," I agreed, "so it's doubtful he has time for much else."

"Well, we'll find out soon. We're going to ask for a Leonard Bernstein Department, funded by CBS. If they accept, they can distribute what they refer to as my 'product' . . . and I intend to do everything in video and audio. If they turn us down, we'll go over to the Germans—who have made us a generous offer."

I was sitting there in institutional air-conditioned darkness at midday in the Ohio summer, trying to dope it out, like why is this icon sitting here telling me his business secrets? And generally: what's up? Of course, he sensed my confusion, and clued me in:

"So, I'd like to discuss hiring you to run this new division, should they show the good sense to accept our proposal."

YES!!

"And why are you asking me?"

I guess I really couldn't finally accept that this casual meeting with a local Cleveland broadcaster was seriously intended.

"You must know that I was impressed with what you said yesterday . . . and of course there was that time in the '60s. . . ."

EASY, BIG FELLA, I was telling myself.

". . . and when you asked about a new *West Side Story* I started thinking maybe you're the person to help me get to a project like that, find a suitable—relevant—script. Could you even write something yourself?"

IS HE ASKING ME?

"So I'm offering you a many-faceted job: produce my worldwide tours and recordings, look out for my interests at CBS, and help me find a book from which to make a socially valuable theater piece for the present political circumstances. All conditional upon Clive's acceptance of our proposition."

"He'd be a fool to turn you down."

"Turn *us* down," he ventured in friendship, "and," he grinned, "Mr. Davis would certainly seem to qualify."

We talked for two more hours. I spent that weekend in and out of his dressing room at Blossom Center, watching him rehearse the mighty *Resurrection Symphony* by his predecessor Jewish composer/conductor, the immortal Gustav Mahler.

Finally, Saturday night, soprano and alto soloists, Cleveland Orchestra, and chorus filled the humid Summit County air with a message to George Szell's distant but abiding spirit:

O glaube, mein Herz, o glaube,
es geht dir nichts verloren!
Dein ist, was du gesehnt,
dein was du geliebt,
was du gestritten!

(O believe, my heart
that no trace of you will be lost!

What you longed for is yours forever;
What you loved and would have given your life for!)

When we'd parted Bernstein had asked for some of my writing and accepted my offer to write a *dona nobis pacem*—a peace poem—for his just-commissioned "Mass" for the opening of Kennedy Center. I dashed off some sample verses in what I thought was simple rhythmic popular style, based on the image of all generations of mankind inhabiting the Earth simultaneously, since at any given moment, the bomb could expunge past, present and future in a single MIRV.

It wasn't bad.

Soon I had a letter from the head of Lenny's New York-based production company confirming our potential relationship:

"Lenny has told us about you and I'm delighted to. . . ."

But later, one from the Maestro himself, from Vienna:

"I went to see Clive personally. I'm sorry to say he all but said, 'Lenny who?' I fear our enterprise together is at an end. I start talks with Die Deutscher next Tuesday. Thanks, B."

By the time I received this fateful communique I had become fairly well entrenched at one of the new breed called "progressive rock" stations that had surfaced in Cleveland, with my own air shift as well as an hour weekly interview show. In the fullness of time Clive Davis was fired as President of Columbia Records for allegedly spending company funds on his son's ultra-Bar Mitzvah (later, of course, to scale the heights of record-biz réclame, most recently winning multiple Grammys for Carlos Santana). "The Germans," as Lenny called them, went laughing all the way to the Deutschbank with the residuals from Bernstein CDs, laserdiscs, and tapes. And I became a radio "personality" in what was becoming AOR—Album-Oriented Rock.

As painstakingly elaborated above, I was on fire again for the new liberating spirit and ideas of the late '60s and early '70s. As Public Service Director of WNCR and WMMS in Cleveland I interviewed a lot of the people in the hopeful anecdotes above, as I allowed "the counterculture" simply to sweep me away in a new social direction altogether. My talk show featured guests like Pierre Salinger, Dennis Kucinich, Isaac Asimov, and many heroes of rock 'n' roll.

With the aborting of the Bernstein project I ceased looking Eastward to Europe (through the prism of New York) and redirected my attention toward California, with its cultural diversity and fabled openness of mind. In Los Angeles I would do hundreds of interviews—in public and commercial radio and television—and find the education that only an interview can, if it succeeds, provide.

8

Media Formats

Skip this chapter if—and only if—you've already figured out that "an interview is an interview," and that you can work out for yourself what size, shape, and form your interview will take, regardless of the medium. What's the big deal?

Consider this: although interviews are essentially identical at their core, the ways they are used by the various media can be diverse.

As the first edition of this book was being written, Tina Brown's (*Vanity Fair*, *The New Yorker*) new magazine, *Talk*, was sold out on Los Angeles newsstands because its first issue, with its "Interview with Hillary Rodham Clinton" was so hot; the mag was flying off shelves from Century City to North Hollywood. And the *Playboy* interview with Minnesota Governor Jesse Ventura created such a major media/congressional stinkorama that the *Playboy* interviewer, Lawrence Grobel, was himself deluged by requests for interviews by every mainstream media outlet in America. *Playboy* then repackaged the issue in a plastic wrapper with red letters that shouted: "JESSE 'THE INTERVIEW' VENTURA." Just two more examples that interviews (even in the presumably superannuated print medium) are here to stay.

Whether conducted by columnist, anchor, field reporter, or "other," interviews—as a form or an event—seem permanently imbedded in our culture. Every kind of medium today calls for interviews, fast and furious. I've even done them for CD-ROM, electronic press kits, and music videos. From high school newspaper to the World Wide Web, interviews are cheap, often entertaining, and—at their best—revealing.

But (to meddle with an old cliché), the more things change externally, the more their core remains the same. An interview, by Aristotle or *Playboy*, is an interview. But, despite many similarities, interviews must conform to the wrinkles of each medium. Let's examine the most important of these, starting with the most basic: words on paper.

Print

We start with the requirements of the print medium, because they are the easiest to understand technically, even though they can be the hardest in the long haul, and most demanding. Also, print (along with college and community/cable radio and TV) is open more often to beginning interviewers (and controversial subjects) than the more costly professional broadcast media.

Although they are far lower in the editorial content mix than in broadcast media, print interviews, with their trademark Q's and A's, still find significant favor with editors and readers alike. Consider: the groundbreaking institution, the *Playboy* Interview, which, after 40 years, is still prestigious enough to have its guest blurbed on the magazine's cover; Andy Warhol's *Interview*, which includes in its current issue (as I write this) no less than seven feature interviews; Robert Scheer's late, lamented political interviews not too long ago in the *Los Angeles Times*; and the abovementioned Hillary Clinton feature in *Talk*.

The good news about print is its ease of editing. It's the obvious truth about any recorded interview, that you can tape-record gigantic chunks of time and later, in splendid isolation, omit whatever doesn't meet content or space requirements. The intermediate step, in many cases, is to have the recorded interview transcribed, or do it yourself, and then do the editing from hard copy: words on paper. Printed.

With a transcription before you, you can scan the entire interview at a glance, thus avoiding forwarding and reversing your way through an hour or two of cassette tape (or data in whatever form), or page-upping and -downing an endless caravan of computer screens. But it's your choice.

Print interviews can be brilliant stand-alones in themselves (as the original *Playboy* interviewer's, Charlotte Chandler's, always were), but usually require the addition of a few well-chosen words of introduction. You might consider occasional interstitial sentences (or even paragraphs) as explanation and general enhancement. Novelistic devices such as a sense of location, description of the subject's mannerisms, appearance, tone of voice, etc., help make more effective copy, or a finished story, depending on your goal.

On the other hand I've occasionally sold raw, unedited radio interviews to various publications, which cut them to fit their own needs, leaving whatever writing to staff people. But in general, the better you write, the better your print interview will be.

In the mid '90s I hosted an interview with Native American activist and actor Russell Means, whose book, *Where White Men Fear to Tread*, had just been published. A poetry-based California coffeehouse publication asked me to interview Means, whose heroism on behalf of AIM and charismatic acting (in Oliver Stone's *The Doors*, among others) I'd greatly admired; but whose nationalism/exclusionism, as put forward in the book, I found hard to take, however "understandable" as a reaction to historic oppression.

Driving over to his house I conjured a vision of my youthful but politically inert editor and figured he could, with a little creative editing, use only the more savory Q's and A's, and consign what I considered the counterproductive race-baiting to the editorial wastebasket. Then my conscience made an emergency landing on my shoulder. "No," it told me. "Why are you assuming the worst from your editor? Isn't that exactly what you always inveigh against: cutting the material to fit preconceived notions?"

In the end, rather than simply let his racism go unanswered, and later simply editing it out for political expediency, I jumped in and debated the imposing actor/activist (as politely as possible) into the night. Ultimately the interview took two full 60-minute cassettes, and, as far as I know, looked great in print, regardless.

Broadcast (Taped and Live)

Despite the triumph of soundbites on evening news shows and elsewhere, there is a countercurrent building of television and radio shows that increasingly use interviews longer than ten seconds. Reality, investigative, or documentary shows—like BBC America's *Hard Talk*, *60 Minutes*, PBS's *Frontline*, Bill Moyers' many excellent series, and others—require good, hard-hitting interrogatory/expository interviews. These are often, as you probably know, longer interviews, which are cut up as needed and blended with narration (on and/or off-camera) by an anchor, and other elements to tell a particular story.

Historically the greatest opportunity (and audience) for in-depth interviewing has come from cultural programming. These are of two distinct types:

External/Objective: e.g., MTV, E! The Entertainment Channel, or most morning and other talk shows, where creative people, sports stars, and/or public figures focus on their careers, new releases, fashion, gossip, industry rumors, all valuable cultural/historical data; and

Internal/Subjective: e.g., Bravo's two brilliant series *Inside the Actors Studio* and *Bravo Profiles* with British writer/producer Melvin Bragg. Also CBS/Discovery-People Channel series, which gave us, for example, Mike Wallace's revealing talk with Arthur Miller, in which the playwright admits being shattered by every subsequent review after (and despite) the abiding success of *Death of a Salesman*.

In the late '70s I worked on one of the first network music shows, *The Midnight Special* for NBC-TV. One of my duties on the 90-minute late-night hit show was to oversee the weekly "Salute" sections, 10- to 15-minute biographies of great pop musicians. At the time, the legendary Jerry Lee Lewis was making the first of many comebacks, after his scandalous marriage to an underage cousin.

My coworker, the fabulous Tisha Fein, was doing the actual interview, as she always did when male musicians were the guests (i.e., most of the time), as I stood quietly by in support. When Tisha had asked the last of her questions, the subject everyone was dying to hear about had not been broached. We had the three-camera crew for only a few more minutes. Tisha stared at me imploringly.

So I stepped forward:

"Killer," I began, pausing to let this respectful salutation take effect, "what were you thinking when you married your 13-year-old cousin and took her on tour with you to London?"

There was quiet on the set. Jerry Lee looked at me like he'd just seen a snake. Behind the piano his face was contracting ominously. Suddenly, looking directly at me, he sprang to his feet, sending the piano bench flying backwards with a bang! and thundered:

"That's right! That's right!" pounding the piano for punctuation, then shaking his fist at me with patented ferocity. "That's right! Everyone said she was 13! *The London Times! The New York Times!*" He snarled. "But not one of 'em! Not *one* mentioned that she turned 14 the very next *week*!"

And another freeze frame.

Interview Specials (Network/Local)

There are times when the broadcast interview, as such, is brought front-and-center in all its glory. These are the taped radio and (mostly) TV specials networks air to meet the demands of a specific occasion: from serious-minded programs, like David Frost's series with Richard Nixon, to timely and commerce-driven shows, like the victorious General Colin Powell to Anyone Who Knew Princess Di, or Martha Stewart. They all offer looks at how uniquely exciting, revealing, and enlightening an interview can be.

Not that they always deliver the goods in real life. Limits of every kind can be brought to bear on these occasions. Certain topics may be prohibited; many, if not all, of the questions will be agreed upon in advance. The limits are often set by handlers. The subject himself or herself, acting through a publicist, is often given final cut. And so forth.

Nevertheless, a certain amount of valuable material manages to get through to the enormous audiences these specials usually draw. The body language. Phrasing. Telltale pauses and stutters. The way the guest handles questions: directly, or "Let me say this about that. . ." Subtle but relevant details that require attention from the audience.

Then there's technique. Whatever you may think of Barbara Walters and her network colleagues as original thinkers, scholars, or depth psychologists—or even broadcast journalists—they know their way around interview form and are a joy to watch at the purely mechanical level. Much can be learned from these jamborees, where "the whole world is watching," or at least an almost Super Bowl-sized audience. The pressure is on big-time, and they always seem to respond like the pros they are. They wouldn't be there if their techniques weren't flawless. Technique is a given at these levels. AND they have sizeable staffs.

Local Specials

In local markets independent interviews stand some chance of reaching the air, but local news reporters usually have the inside track. So it may be more provident to hone your interview techniques, hire on at an independent station as a reporter, and go from there. For beginners, many stations offer intern jobs, where you can begin to learn these skills (in addition to the irreplaceable lessons of this book, of course).

Quickies: Featurettes and Sound Bites

Many people look down their noses at featurettes. But short, pithy programs, like the series "Minutes On" (pieces on travel, wine, investing, etc.) that *The New York Times* used to offer, featuring the paper's own columnist on the topic in question, can sometimes do a better job than longer, weighty programming on the same topic. The secret is compression. Get it on, and get it over.

Over the last decade I've been producing and hosting a series of two-minute featurettes for classical-music radio called *Martin Perlich Interviews*. The show airs weekdays, three times a day, during morning and afternoon drive-time and at noon. The guest is a major classical music performer, conductor, or composer, and, being based in Los Angeles, I've seldom had problems rounding up world-class guests: Kiri Te Kanawa, Isaac Stern, Kathleen Battle, Sir Yehudi Menuhin, and many more.

I sit down with my subjects in a variety of locations: backstage at the L.A. Music Center, the Hollywood Bowl, dressing rooms, hotel rooms, or in the studio. I've even done conductor/pianist/composer Andre Previn over breakfast at the Four Seasons.

Once the interview—between 30 minutes and 2 hours—is on tape, I transfer it to the digital editor (in the beginning reel-to-reel, of course) and cut five 90-second shows (Monday, violin superstar Itzhak Perlman on Mozart; Tuesday, on his childhood training in Israel; Wednesday, on his disability, and so on), so that a regular drive-time listener is presented a series of snapshots of the many aspects of an artist, which, in the end, offer an aggregate, a compressed portrait. I also write and voice the intros and outros for the show, each of which contains maybe 90 seconds of actual interview. The show was honored by the International Radio Festival of New York two years in a row. The show was recently picked up for syndication, which demonstrates how someone working locally can not only *effect* things globally, but *broadcast* globally as well. As of this writing, *Martin Perlich Interviews* airs three times every weekday on public radio station KCSN 88.5, Northridge/Los Angeles, and on the Web at www.kcsn.org.

With the possible exception of field interviews at sites of wars, tornadoes, and other tragedies (usually done by seasoned reporters, who also provide a location "standup"), sound bites are mostly superficial and misleading. This justly maligned format usually presents only the conventional wisdoms, or "CWs" as Robert Parry calls them in his 1992 book, *Fooling America*, which "merely reinforce the dominant attitude of the moment." This applies, unfortunately, to much of big-time broadcasting, radio, and TV. From NPR to CNN, from local markets to network news, wherever they hold sway, sound bites can usually only illustrate a prepared narrative, not report an event in the depth required to contextualize it, and thereby make it real.

The assignment editor and/or field producer may have already decided what they want. They may tell you in advance, sometimes almost word-for-word, what is needed, often on the basis of images they've already planned or shot, or a "spin" already decided upon by policymakers above your AND their heads. This is usually tough to fight. You will probably decide that you can only do the best job possible, your best shot given the limitations. The alternative is to try to gather whatever additional interview material you decide independently is of importance to the story, and risk your job to get it aired. Needless to say, this is very rare. Keeping your résumé updated is advised.

Though sound-bite gathering has too often become a job of harvesting, plain and simple, it is never inappropriate to pick the best fruit, as it were. Professionalism is Job One. Establish your credibility by being prepared, concise, on time, discriminating in your fact-selection, and well-spoken. Personality, where it is not forbidden, is sometimes a welcome addition. Remember: better opportunities may present themselves later. Or you may get sucked up into the system of "fooling America" and decide it's the best you can do with your life. In either case, do it well. If you find yourself in this position, follow their lead, be prompt and courteous. Give them their CW. Have a nice day.

Investigative Interviews: *Caveant Omnes*

Investigative interviewing should best be left to trained investigative journalists, well-versed in the ins and outs of the law, public records, privacy considerations, and hand-to-hand combat. The staffs and crews of the big network shows like *60 Minutes*, *Hard Copy*, *20/20*, et al., have lawyers on retainer and burly grips, best boys, and others who can protect them from the inevitable resistance that people with something to hide seek to raise when you start acting like Dustin Hoffman/Robert Redford in *All the President's Men* or Al Pacino in *The Insider*.

All the tricks of hidden cameras, in-your-face microphones, impromptu set-to's with executives like Phil Knight of Nike—much less wiretapping, sniffing around people's garbage, and the elaborate con games that investigative reporters sometimes have to employ—lie well beyond the scope of this book, and should not be undertaken light-mindedly.

Live

Live means actually live, of course. No safety net, no editing, no stopping tape, no Take Two. The dangers here are many. For example:

Stan Harris, our wonderful veteran director on *The Midnight Special*, told me he was shooting jazz diva Sarah Vaughan absolutely live for the short-lived late-'80s TV show called *Live from 8-H* from NBC's famous studio of that name. Halfway through the show, "Sassy" didn't like what she was hearing, and started waving for Stan's attention. "Stop tape! Stop tape!" she demanded, as the seconds ticked by in silence. Ultimately they went to commercial, and Stan took a nice vacation.

Ask any sports fan the difference between watching a game live or "tape-delayed." There is a quality to live events. Imagine Randy Johnson throwing low and outside, and the director calling, "Take it again: The sponsor wants it over the plate." Remember, there is one quality that all live events share—chance.

In the early '80s I was working in development at KCET, the Los Angeles public television station. My company was brought in specifically to bring younger, "hipper" audiences to PBS, whose average viewer age was 70-something, and we were set to work on specials for Stevie Wonder, Jackson Browne, a documentary on Music and the '60s, and a few other Boomer-oriented shows.

But one of my favorite projects was a live drama series, developed primarily by my partner, called *Hollywood 90*. The show harked back to the early days of television, especially the brilliant early live drama series like *Playhouse 90*, *Kraft Theater*, *Philco Playhouse*, and other regular live drama programs from TV's Golden Age, the '50s.

We had interested some of the gifted original live-TV directors in getting back in the saddle for us, and more importantly had lined up major stars. For example, for our first show, we had Robert DeNiro set to play Duke Mantee in *The Petrified Forest*—broadcast live from our soundstages in L.A. Everywhere we went, people were jumping up and down with enthusiasm. Cable TV was in its infancy, but HBO gave strong indications of wanting to partner with us, and the KCET underwriting (sales) department was saying they had sponsorship very interested.

But as the project accelerated, we began to experience resistance. And in a final climactic meeting with the program managers, we were finally told, in no uncertain terms, that they were "scared of doing it live."

"What if something goes wrong?" they wanted to know.

"Not to worry. They're actors," I reminded them, "They'll think of something." The project was allowed to fizzle.

But that wasn't the point. There is to live performing an adrenal quality that is irreplaceable, unrepeatable, and unbeatable. Ask any jazz musician. Bureaucrats have a hard time sympathizing with our appreciation for live broadcasting—radio or TV. They prefer the predictability of canned. But the performers know. And, in the final analysis, so do audiences.

The most definitive statement of the cultural value of live performance I know is the answer Cleveland Orchestra Musical Director George Szell gave me in the first of our many interviews to open the seven consecutive Cleveland Orchestra syndicated broadcast seasons where I was Intermission Host.

The day of the interview I had happened upon an article in *High Fidelity* by the great Canadian pianist Glenn Gould, who had just retired from public performance. In the article Gould proclaimed that, with the advent of the LP record, live concerts were on the way out. In the future, music would be made primarily in the studio, where tapes could be edited to give the audience the perfection it deserved.

Somehow it occurred to me to ask Mr. Szell to comment on Gould's controversial premise. He gazed off for a long moment, and then spoke quietly, looking directly into my eyes. "First of all, I should say I'm no prophet." I nodded in tentative accord, as he continued, "but I should like to hope, that in the future [pause] when you have an orchestra of, say, 100 players, and perhaps a chorus, and soloists, and everything might go wrong [pause] but in the grace of the moment, it does not. I should hope that moments like that should be of lasting value to the community of listeners."

The grace of the moment.

So, hats off to Larry King, who does a live show every day. To the battalion of sportscasters who do live sideline, locker room, courtside, and other catch-as-catch-can interviews on the fly. To Amy Goodman at *Democracy Now!* who chases down duplicitous politicos for interrogations as they try to beg off; and Christiane Amanpour and her colleagues in the field, who report from the world's front lines, tossing off live interviews with bombing victims, refugees, government officials, etc., and all the time staying in sync with their network anchors, hitting commercial breaks on time, and all the constraints of live broadcast. And finally, hats off to the few remaining live-concert, opera, or other event intermission interviewers working against time requirements, chasing down star performers, etc., who nevertheless manage to ask the right question: bravi tutti.

Talk Shows, Call-Ins, and *Oprah*

An entire industry has sprung up around humans talking to each other via broadcast transmitters while other humans listen in. Despite the richly deserved criticism talk shows have gotten from the mainstream press, consider the alternative: the sound of silence. It is our constitutional right to give free expression to our ideas, and talk shows, call-in shows, and phone interviews for radio and TV are merely a logical extension of this right, amplified by technology.

Which doesn't mean it's all good, socially valuable, democratic, or even entertaining. Corporate control and fundamentalist religion have taken their toll. By far the best, in terms of audience enrichment/enlightenment, was the Old Oprah, whose open-hearted and sincere love of literature combined with her skills as a fine actress to make her a more influential patron of the arts than all of the Medici combined.

But, alas, more usually it's some sad hater of a guy with a way-limited worldview trying to impose his bitterness-induced (and Right Wing-financed?) construction of reality on a residuum of loyal listeners—for a living. All what's remarkable about this is how and where they find people willing to phone up a Rush Limbaugh-type and be squashed like little bugs for disagreeing with the omniscient host/tormenter. Strange. But I guess when those sufficiently gluttonous for punishment have had their fill of public humiliation, they are ready to be guests on *Springer*.

By now, a number of variants of the talk show have shot up like wild turnips on radio and television, each presenting yet another variation on the theme of human communication; and each calling for a skillful host, familiar with the call-and-response patterns of the interview form.

Watch CNN's Joie Chen seamlessly turn from a live General Somebody in-studio to a still of a foreign correspondent speaking live by phone from Someplace Exotic to a video feed of Wolf Blitzer at the White House or Somebody Else on Wall Street. The fundamental skill here is listening. No matter how well-prepared you (or your staff, in the case of any network, or even local anchor) are, the Tao of this situation is to assimilate each guest's response and to respond to it in the form of a question to another guest.

Listening, brothers and sisters. These anchors are no longer simple news readers as they have been for decades. No, the role of interviewer—driven by the never-ending spurts of technological advances, has evolved into that of a broadcast ring-mistress. Not only do they have to keep three or four guests from straying from the subject, or eating each other alive (as rapier-tongued columnist Christopher Hitchens did to poor unsuspecting Charlton Heston during coverage of the Gulf War) but they must make it look easy, and hit the commercial break on the nose, as well.

I personally have not worked extensively in call-in situations, but I do know the power of the format, from one of the few listener phone-in shows I found memorable: the night Bobby Kennedy was assassinated. I was about to do my usual *Perlich Project* show (an early prototype for the popular L.A. public-radio show *Morning Becomes Eclectic*), playing everything from Alan Ginsberg to Mozart, Lenny Bruce to Frank Zappa, and lots in between. On the drive to the studio the word came from Los Angeles that RFK had been shot down, so I just naturally asked the engineer to patch my phone on-air. And we took phone calls. Many years later, when I met Devo, one of the Bobs told me that he'd heard that show and never forgotten it.

Not that I was any good at it, or that every show is slated to be "meaningful." It's just the impulse: to be there when people need to express themselves. In this case it was a great national calamity. But every day is a calamity for someone, and it can help us all to have these outlets handy when they are needed. Despite their famously wretched excesses, I salute the men and women who do this very stressful work. They are members of the helping professions, whatever their motives. Or could be—in a perfect world.

Live Event Coverage: Concerts and Games

In one sense, live event coverage is easy: any minor fluffs and blunders you might make only add to the "liveness" of the broadcast, and your own "humanness" as an interviewer. Of course, there are limits. No audience will sit still for a stumblebum interlocutor, full of "uh"s and "duh"s and long silences. Neither will an employer. But, within reason, the adrenal rush you'll get from a live event—knowing there is no tomorrow—can raise the level of your performance to unaccustomed heights.

Though jazz great Miles Davis never made a "mistake" as such, he played a lot of egregious "wrong" notes, which caused musical problems, which in turn only inspired him to find greater creative "solutions" to them. This was a key element in his unique style of improvisation. Think of yourself as one of the performers—one of the lead singers or quarterbacks you're interviewing backstage or on the sidelines, and pick up their now-or-never energy.

The very first time I did a live symphony concert it was—as first times often are—as emergency fill-in for the regular guy. Arriving early at the imposing L.A.-area concert hall, I was presented with what I thought was an odd set-up. They were performing the Second Symphony of Gustav Mahler, which calls for soloists, a huge chorus, and full symphony orchestra. The stage would be jammed. But, instead of sitting offstage in a broadcast booth, where I could rehearse to my heart's content, kick back, and relax off-mic while the music played, I found that I was to sit onstage with the performers, where I couldn't even dare to rustle my script.

Oh, well. No turning back. I was here and I'd do my best. My job was to host the entire broadcast: opening welcome, program notes on each of the pieces, translate/explain key sections of the German text of the Mahler, and do a closing interview with the well-known conductor at the end of the concert. Quite a load for my first live-concert assignment and with less than a day's notice.

I found my way nervously to the back of the stage and carefully gathered my notes as orchestra members set up all around me and a 150-voice chorus filed in behind my little desk. My producer appeared from nowhere and pointed at me.

"You're on."

I hadn't even put on my headset, but did so belatedly and started my opening spiel. "Good evening and welcome . . ." (You know the drill). Then I remembered that it was my job to vamp till ready; read my program notes until the conductor took the podium, no matter how long or short a time that turned out to be. I looked around anxiously for the conductor. No Maestro. Again. No. Again. Not yet.

At a time like that you simply throw away the script and let yourself go. I took a deep breath, started improvising into contiguous universes of discourse, and somehow managed to stre-e-e-e-tch my intro for another four or five whole minutes, until—at last!—our Maestro took to the stage. The huge audience applauded his entrance, the music began, and I could finally stop talking.

Everything went well until just before the end of the broadcast. Because I was so relaxed from the success of my pre-concert exertions, I figured the rest of my chores would be a veritable piece o' cake. And they were, as it turned out, pretty straightforward. But I discovered I still had one last duty: to conduct a post-concert interview with our conductor at the end and pitch back to the studio.

The concert's final notes were sounding, the bravos ringing out through the hall, bows being taken, when I heard my producer's voice in my "cans":

"Maestro can't do the interview; try to get the soprano instead."

Never mind that, although she'd sung at the Met, I barely knew her name, much less career highlights. *Plus*—did she know the drill? And, if not, was I supposed to grab her as she trotted by at the same time doing the concluding announce? Apparently.

In moments like these it's good to have a handy Plan B. When you go "live," you've already crossed the border into improvland. So, I simply grabbed the mic and took off in search of the peripatetic singer, explaining my every move to the audience to cover the inevitable delay. Catching up with her backstage (luckily the cable was long enough) I simply avoided her career (which I didn't know) and addressed my questions to Mahler's written text (which I *did* know). To this day I can't quite believe it worked. But it was my "live" attitude, my "came-to-play" approach that made it work. Ready to scramble, on the one hand; and not afraid of making a "mistake" on the other. Live is live—period.

Other Mutants

A weird sort of hybrid is the live interview before an audience. You're neither a moderator, exactly, nor an MC. You're assigned a prominent figure to debrief in public, while someone may even tape the occasion, on audio or video, or both; e.g., a film curator briefly interviews a director or star before a screening of his/her film. Or consider the following example:

Not too long ago a prominent Los Angeles classical radio host asked me to fill in for him at the last minute. The gig was to interview the acclaimed tenor José Carreras—one of The Three Tenors—before an invited group of society people and other music lovers at a fancy Beverly Hills hotel. I'd always wanted to meet the only one of the Fab Three I'd never interviewed. Plus, Señor Carreras had conquered a vicious form of cancer and had restarted his career soon after leaving the hospital. An exciting opportunity with inspirational questions just begging to be asked. Plus there was a fee involved.

I wasn't working in music at the time, hadn't done an interview in a long while, and so boning up was indicated. I spent an entire weekend catching up on Carreras' recordings, watching his videos (including Leonard Bernstein getting on his case for an un-American accent in the all-star recording of *West Side Story*), and read everything about his struggle with chemotherapy and worse.

By the night of the interview I arrived with a file full of notes. Skirting the valet parkers, I found myself a room off the small auditorium we were using, and sat down for a final look at my research.

The file was bulky, so I winnowed out what I needed and left the extraneous material in a separate folder. In due time Señor Carreras came in to be introduced. I was enjoying myself chatting with him about favorite tenors, and when the video crew called us to enter before a packed hall, I reached down for my notes, and—of course—in the absence of grace in the moment, picked up the wrong file.

It wasn't till we were sitting in our overstuffed chairs under the lights that I realized my error. Was there time to pop up and sprint to retrieve the right notes? I'd written at least 15 questions . . .

The head of the sponsoring group was finishing his intro. I looked up at the video people. Tape was rolling. I chose (a strong word) to sit it out. But my "choice" was made of confusion and fear. As a result of my gutlessness, the opening of the interview was professionally embarrassing.

Bumbling through a well-memorized but inadequately pre-structured bio of Carreras, I was weighed down by my own ineptitude. The audience didn't seem to be noticing. Luckily the next higher level of adrenaline soon kicked in to drive the panic away, and at last I ended my Homer Simpson imitation. Thus energized, I conducted an interview that was (except for the beginning) actually better than it might have been with notes.

This example illustrates two points: live interviews are perilous, especially with the audience present and staring at you, and that while presence of mind may be able to save you when all else fails, it is better to be prepared. And that, as we have just seen, does not mean just research.

9

Troubleshooting

I approach these questions unwillingly, as they are sore subjects,
but no cure can be effected without touching upon
and handling them.
—Titus Livius (59 B.C.–17 A.D.)

Every high endeavor meets with some resistance from the world—from traffic jams to mechanical failures, from mixed signals to crossed wires. You will learn more from your trials than you will from your successes, but there's no reason to give your difficulties any help. Here are some situations that I went through that can show you how a sense of flexibility and humility can go a long way toward warding off disaster.

The Late Mr. Host

Sometimes YOU WILL BE LATE. Despite all your preparation, your best intentions, your skillful navigating, and the propitiation of the gods, you will find yourself stuck in traffic, lost, or otherwise detained. This is why the universe sent us cell phones. Call ahead. You're "running late." Approximate your ETA for your guest and take a deep breath. A credible-sounding excuse, sincerely tendered, will almost always suffice.

Full disclosure: I do not own a cell phone. Call it superstition, Luddism, old-fashioned obstinacy, or whatever. I just don't. Sometimes I suffer for my reluctance stubbornness. To wit:

I got a call at home that my request for an interview with Leonard Nimoy had been accepted; could I get to his home by 2:00? "Of course" is the standard interviewer riposte. But it was noon. I'd have to drive a half hour to the radio station, where the mini-disc player I use was being used by my GM. I can still make it, I figured. But when I had to wait an hour for the unit to be charged and packed up, I could feel something toxic starting to drip-drip-drip into my stomach. Still, when I mounted my aged Volvo I had a half hour to get to Mr. Nimoy's sylvan retreat in the Bel Air Estates—if I could find it from the directions the publicist had sent me. Then, of course, it became immediately apparent that the 405 Freeway was determined to be its baddest self. I watched with growing dismay as the clock ticked toward 2:00. I struggled to master my mind: I didn't even *like* Leonard Nimoy; had never watched more than a few cursory minutes of his Mr. Spockness, so admired by millions. No offense—I was just not there for *Star Trek*; had been an adult when it first aired, and missed the trance that it had spun to capture so many younger viewers in its thrall. So where did that leave me? I was doing the interview because Nimoy was performing with the L.A. Philharmonic. Esa-Pekka Salonen had cast him in the role of Narrator in one of the scariest, most moving monodramas in all of music: *A Survivor from Warsaw* set against the nightmarish dissonances of Arnold Schönberg's music.

2:10. Wish I had a cell phone.

The freeway begins to move. I exit at Sunset, paddle the old car past the UCLA traffic, find the correct Bel Air gate, hunt the house. FINALLY turn off into tree-shaded mansion. Here goes nuttin. Nimoy meets me at the door.

"A thousand pardons," I say, "the 405 was . . ."

He waves me into silence. Everyone who's visited Southern California knows the feared and reviled San Diego Freeway, Highway 405. So Nimoy was cool with it, waving me in. As I fumble to set up (the recorder had not taken the charge), my mind is a loose confederation of floating particles. Finally, I push RECORD and when I look up I realize: "There is something about this man I really like; has he actually *become* the beloved Spock?"

We talk about *Survivor of Warsaw* briefly, and then off into what made him an actor: a teenage chance to play in a play by Clifford Odets, a calling to do good through art, a life in theatre.

An hour later he was walking me out to my car. "An old Volvo, eh?" he said and smiled.

The Hostile Guest

As long as there are interviews there will be the occasional hostile subject. Not just those who bridle when you unfurl your "hard question," but guests with attitude. They're out there. And they're no pleasure, because the job's hard enough without sudden shocks to the limbic system.

Make no mistake: yours may be the thirtieth microphone or camera crew your subject has faced that week, or in your city, or just that day. Attitude may arise simply from exhaustion, boredom with a publicity tour, a bad sales report, or the naturally bilious response to repeating the same answer to the same question. The subject is not the problem. You are there to get an interview, regardless of attitude.

Of course you approach each interview with the dedication to pull the highest level of mind out of your subject. At the same time, deep in some crevice of your subconscious, you must be prepared for the worst. You must have an onboard lawyer, who's already assessed the worst-case scenario for you and is locked and loaded.

My first and most difficult hostile subject was the brilliant young pianist Peter Serkin, who, in 1969, was still known primarily as the son of revered piano master Rudolf Serkin. I was the equally youthful Intermission Host of *The Cleveland Orchestra Concerts* series, interviewing a never-ending caravan of glittering guest soloists, conductors, and composers, all come to make music with Maestro Szell and/or his world-champion orchestra.

Spring 1969: The Vietnam War was raging. Young Serkin was guest soloist of the week. I waited for him in the broadcast booth high atop Severance Hall. He arrived late, grumped hello without meeting my eyes, and slumped into the guest's chair. Uh-oh. I essayed to chat him up. He responded in grunts and other monosyllables. The producer called out "tape is rolling" and off we went.

I began with questions about the Mozart concerto he was playing. "I don't want to talk about that," he informed me. What about his father's influence? Same answer. A few more queries. Same answer. "Well, Peter, what *would* you like to talk about?"

"The war," he said. There it was. Finally.

Without even stopping tape I explained the obvious: that while I might agree with his opposition to the war, this was a taped interview and anything as divisive as a discussion of the war in Southeast Asia would never make it onto the air.

He seemed to understand. I started again. "What would you like to talk about?"

"Ice cream."

For the first time in my career I simply gave up. Knew I was licked. And, certain that we had enough tape in our archives to cover us for that week, I thanked him and walked out.

Not a great strategy, I confess, nor would I advocate it in most cases, but you have to face the fact that sometimes—despite your best efforts—an interview simply doesn't "happen."

Peter Serkin, of course, has become one of our best pianists, especially as the champion of modern composers, and the music of Bach and Mozart. Although I never second-guessed my own actions on that occasion, I always regretted that it happened, and of course respected Peter's attempt to use his position to give voice to his beliefs, however ineffective the vehicle of expression. I have not interviewed him since, but I'm sure that, lacking a cause for hostility, none would emerge. (As it turns out when I queried the L.A. Philharmonic in 2002, I was told, "Mr. Serkin doesn't *do* interviews.")

On the other hand, some subjects are "born with attitude." My favorite example was the late, great Frank Zappa, because, although he always came on sharply skeptical (as opposed to cynical), behind the provocative posture was a deeply thoughtful person, ready and waiting to be engaged if only you asked the right question.

After a shaky start I was able to return, over the next 15 years, for seven more interviews. Yet each time it was necessary to reestablish myself with Frank, duck under the negative neuron-stream, keep my energy up.

Stage Fright: The Golden Pen of Maestro Szell

Sometimes, try as you may, you'll find you can't stop your runaway mouth—especially if you're scared, in awe of your famous and powerful guest. It's not unusual to tend to talk too much when you're nervous, hoping to cover your palpable anxiety. Don't bother. First of all, almost everyone gets stage fright. It's your body's way of getting you ready for a challenge. Secondly, it's transparently obvious.

When I held the job of Intermission Host of the syndicated series *Cleveland Orchestra Concerts*, the orchestra was in its prime, ranked among the best in the world. Its Conductor/Musical Director, George Szell, was widely feared for his icy exterior and tyrannical treatment of players, and widely revered for his encyclopedic knowledge of symphonic literature. It was he who was to be my first interview subject in my new job. Two weeks before the interview, Szell's secretary called: would I please submit a list of ten questions that I intended to ask, for Mr. Szell's prior approval? I had no option but to comply, of course, and any nervousness that I felt had just grown exponentially. "The Bernstein interview might have been a fluke!" I thought.

The appointed day arrived. I was ushered into the old-world elegance of Maestro Szell's sanctum sanctorum, I could feel my knees wobbling, my breath coming in fast, shallow pants. I was 25. My subject had worked in Vienna with the great Richard Strauss himself; had conducted at the Metropolitan Opera and the New York Philharmonic in Carnegie Hall. I was assistant manager of a local record store. I did know Szell's recordings and his career history, but Who Was I?

I shook hands with the stately Mr. Szell and sat down. Barely able to meet his eye, I glanced down at the Maestro's desktop, and—lo, and behold!—what did I see but the Maestro's baton-holding hand, shaking with unease and torturing a gold Mark Cross pen with many foot-pounds of torque. There, before my astonished eyes was this musical legend, bending a $100 writing implement against the elegant Viennese wood surface, until I feared it would literally snap in two! Trembling, pulsing, until "and . . . we're rolling" saved us both.

Don't be intimidated by reputation or personal regard. Behind every legend is a person just like yourself, and they may be more nervous about talking to you than you are about talking to them.

10

Re-Viewing the Interview

Luck is what happens when preparation meets opportunity.
—Seneca (4 B.C.–65 A.D.)

Interview as Occupation

The job of interviewing is a would-be Renaissance man or woman's dream come true. You get to meet people from every conceivable walk of life, at all different points in their journeys and at different levels of success (or failure), and get paid for learning about them, relating to them, and then passing that information on to others. What other career allows you to explore the best (or at least the breadth) of human-kind in such a way that brings value to you (in the form of both experience and money) to them, and to the infinite number of audience members who may come across what you've documented? Sometimes a seemingly small assignment will have huge implications; sometimes it's practice for an upcoming challenge. But the job of interviewer can stay fresh for a lifetime.

Interview as Science

There is a science to interviewing that is at play no matter how intuitively one is able to arrive at it. The action/reaction of questioning and the answers it provokes, the chemistry of the emotions (both for the subject and the interviewer), and the accuracy needed to deliver the data—these aspects can all be mapped and charted. To treat your role with care—even meticulousness—can help facilitate the higher levels of the interview process.

Interview as Art

Finally, be assured: a great interview can "make art." A pretentious formulation, perhaps, for a humble journalistic format currently spreading across all media like a fine mist. But since there is no agreement on the definition of what art is, I humbly and provisionally propose the following elucidation:

Art is the creation of something beautiful where it didn't exist before—moving, insightful, socially valuable, exalting, transcendental—all of these. And, yes, a first-rate interview can meet any or all of these requirements, contain all these qualities, deliver all these essentials.

Do what art does. Look deep into your guests and connect their work with their souls. Yes, souls. Ultimately, communication is about sharing what is true with each other. You, as interviewer, are acting as a conduit between the heart of your subject and the ear of your audience—those you serve. To practice listening for that truth yourself, and then passing it on to others, is the purist element of artistry.

Interviewing Martin Perlich

Q: Martin, do you have anything to say to those who are pondering shoving a mic in the face of a fellow citizen as a career option? An exhortation—or maybe a warning?

A: I, who have questioned, salute you.

Appendix 1

Interviewers of Note

Here we pay tribute to some of those interviewers who have made a contribution to the great tradition of the interview. These outstanding professionals are deeply committed to the mission of interviewing: consistent, career-long dedication to the practices of preparation and listening.

There are many fine interviewers in media today, but these are some of the most prominent—readily available for further observation and study.

Bill Moyers

William Moyers was born in Oklahoma on June 6, 1934, and was raised in Texas. He began his journalism career at age 16 as a cub reporter on the *Marshall News Messenger*.

Moyers has produced more than 200 hours of programming, including *In Search of the Constitution, A Gathering of Men with Robert Bly, Facing Hate with Elie Wiesel, Listening to America with Bill Moyers,* and *Healing and the Mind. Trade Secrets,* Moyers' most recent documentary report, is an investigation of the history of the chemical revolution and the companies that drove it.

Five of Moyers' books based on his television series have become best-sellers, including: *Listening to America, Joseph Campbell and the Power of the Myth, A World of Ideas I and II,* and *Healing and the Mind.*

During his 30 years in the media Moyers has received numerous awards for excellence, including the prestigious Gold Baton from the Alfred I. duPont-Columbia University Broadcast News Awards, and more than 30 Emmy Awards from the National Academy of Television Arts and Sciences. Two of his public television series, *Creativity* and *A Walk Through the 20th Century*, were named the outstanding informational series by the Academy of Arts and Sciences. In 1991, Moyers was elected a Fellow of the American Academy of Arts and Sciences.

Michael Moore

Whatever you think of his politics, you must grant that Michael Moore combines the talents of a crack investigative reporter with the showman's sense of theater. Rather than negating each other, these virtues cross-pollinate, making his interviews uniquely illuminating

Moore was born in 1954 in Davison, Michigan, a suburb of Flint, then home to one of General Motors' biggest manufacturing plants, where Moore's father and grandfather both worked. In high school Moore soon developed an interest in student politics as well as larger issues: he won a merit badge as an Eagle Scout by creating a slide show exposing environmentally unfriendly businesses in Flint. In 1972, when 18-year-olds were granted the right to vote, he ran for a seat on the Flint school board, soon becoming one of the youngest people in the United States to win an election for public office.

Moore began a career as a journalist by working for *The Flint Voice*, an alternative weekly newspaper. In time, he became the editor, and under his leadership the paper expanded into *The Michigan Voice*, one of the most respected alternative political publications in the Midwest. Moore's success at *The Michigan Voice* eventually led to a job offer from *Mother Jones* magazine, where he became editor in 1986. He often butted heads, however, with *Mother Jones'* publishers and management, and after less than a year he was fired.

After a brief spell working with a Ralph Nader organization, Moore got the idea to make a film about his old hometown of Flint and how the local economy had collapsed in the wake of the closure of General Motors' Flint plants despite their continued profitability. In 1989, the completed film *Roger & Me*—in which Moore and his crew repeatedly fail to get General Motors Chairman Roger Smith to agree to an interview—became a major critical success, was honored at a number of film festivals, and went on to become one of the most financially successful documentary features ever made.

Moore participated as an interviewer in the production of *Blood in the Face*, a documentary about extremist white-power groups, and then directed a short follow-up to *Roger & Me*, called *Pets or Meat: The Return to Flint*, which followed what had happened there since the previous film's conclusion. Next, Moore began work on his first fictional feature, *Canadian Bacon*, a satire in which an ineffectual United States president fabricates a "cold war" against Canada. In 1994, Moore took a stab at television with the satiric news and commentary program *TV Nation*, which aired for one season on NBC, and later for two seasons on Fox.

In 1996, Moore returned to the written word, publishing a book of political commentary, *Downsize This!: Random Threats From an Unarmed American*. The book proved to be a surprise bestseller, and as Moore took to the road to promote it, he brought a camera crew along to make a documentary exploring the economic inequality in America as he dashed from city to city; the resultant film, *The Big One*, was released in 1998. In 1999, Moore returned to television with *The Awful Truth*, a blend of comedy and pointed political commentary similar to *TV Nation*.

In the fall of 2001, Moore's next book, *Stupid White Men*, was scheduled for publication when its release was postponed by its publisher, Random House; Moore was openly critical of George W. Bush in the book. According to Moore, Random House was considering canceling the book and destroying its initial print run when he was asked about the book at a convention of library administrators—who promptly launched an e-mail campaign, and in the spring of 2002, *Stupid White Men* was finally released, quickly becoming a major bestseller.

In the fall of 2002, Moore released his fourth feature film, *Bowling for Columbine*, an examination of America's obsession with guns and violence. It was the first documentary to be shown in competition at the Cannes Film Festival in 46 years, and was honored with the festival's Jury Award. Subsequently becoming the most successful documentary in the history of film, *Bowling for Columbine* received an Academy Award for Best Documentary in 2002.

Amy Goodman

Amy Goodman, host of Pacifica's *Democracy Now!,* is a political activist and fearless investigator. She was beaten and thrown out of Indonesia, only to smuggle herself back in to cover East Timor. Sometimes brutally honest, her commitment, skills, and especially her courage are unique in the history of American radio and television.

Amy is a 1998 recipient of the George Polk Award for the radio documentary *Drilling and Killing: Chevron and Nigeria's Oil Dictatorship,* in which she and co-producer Jeremy Scahill exposed the oil company's role in the killing of two Nigerian villagers on May 28, 1998. They were also awarded the Golden Reel for *Best National Documentary* from the National Federation of Community Broadcasters. They also were honored by the Overseas Press Club, a citation they rejected because of the Club's agreement that journalists not question the keynote speaker, U.S. Special Envoy Richard Holbrooke, at the awards dinner, in the midst of the U.S. bombing of Yugoslavia.

Amy has also won numerous awards for the radio documentary she co-produced with journalist Allan Nairn, *Massacre: The Story of East Timor,* including the Robert F. Kennedy Prize for International Reporting, the Alfred I. duPont-Columbia Silver Baton, the Armstrong Award, the Radio/Television News Directors Award, as well as awards from AP, UPI, and the Corporation for Public Broadcasting. In 1991 Goodman and Nairn survived a massacre in East Timor in which Indonesian soldiers gunned down more than 250 Timorese. Amy has reported from Israel and the occupied territories, Cuba, Mexico, Haiti, and was the first journalist ever to interview jailed U.S. citizen Lori Berenson, serving a life sentence in Peru. Goodman also broadcast the first U.S. radio interview with imprisoned East Timor rebel leader Xanana Gusmao. In addition to her daily radio shows, Goodman speaks around the country on university campuses, as well as to human-rights, church, and community groups about media activism. She also runs workshops at community radio stations on grassroots coverage.

James Lipton

James Lipton hosts *Inside the Actors Studio* on the Bravo cable network. He is the textbook example of being prepared. He knows theater, the broader arts world, and much more, yet never seems to come off as snooty, artsy, or too-hip-for-the-room. As director he has developed the therapist's (or interviewer's) touch with actors. Unlike some media druids who treat movie stars as celebrities, Lipton respects and directly addresses their craft, speaking with an intimate, *entre nous* collegiality that slides easily under the egos of the big stars who regularly grace his excellent, insightful show.

Lipton has interviewed more than 80 of contemporary film and theater's most noteworthy contributors. Himself an accomplished director, choreographer, producer, writer of stage and screen, and published author, Mr. Lipton has been instrumental in creating what he refers to as "a unique archive" of in-depth looks at the craft of acting. Notorious for knowing all there is to know about his *Inside The Actors Studio* guests (Sally Field remarked, "Have you been reading my diary? Talking to my shrink?!"), Mr. Lipton spends two weeks vigorously preparing for each interview. The extensive information he and a researcher compile is the basis for his questions, which he then meticulously handwrites himself on hundreds of blue note cards.

Terry Gross

Terry Gross is one of the most familiar voices of public radio. She's the vocal engine for National Public Radio's *Fresh Air,* where she usually interviews two people per day and spends the rest of her time preparing for the next day's guests, reading their books, watching their movies, listening to their music. She began her radio career in 1973 at public-radio station WBFO in Buffalo, New York. There she hosted and produced several arts, women's, and public affairs programs, including *This Is Radio,* a live, three-hour magazine program that aired daily. Two years later, she joined the staff of WHYY-FM in Philadelphia as producer and host of *Fresh Air,* then a local daily interview and music program. In 1985, WHYY-FM launched a weekly half-hour edition of *Fresh Air with Terry Gross,* which was distributed nationally by National Public Radio. Since 1987, a daily one-hour national edition of *Fresh Air* has been produced by WHYY-FM; it now airs on 160 stations. In addition to her work on *Fresh Air,* Gross has served as guest host for the weekday and weekend editions of NPR's *All Things Considered.*

Gross calls radio "a wonderful medium for conversation and for all things related to language . . . because there is nothing visual to distract you. You're not thinking about somebody's hairdo or whether you like their clothes. You are just engaged in what they have to say." Words from a true listener.

Charlie Rose

Charlie Rose is perhaps the best current-affairs interviewer in mainstream media. Well-educated, polite, with broad-ranging interests and economy of expression, he has consistently offered quality access to movers, shakers, and beyond. Perhaps the best example was his show just before the Iraqi War began, when U.S. society was polarized: protesters screaming in the streets, the attack-dogs blasting away from their corporate bully pulpits. Yet there was Charlie with a Left-Right debate between Jonathan Schell of the Nation Institute and Michael Ignatieff of Harvard's Kennedy School, and civility reigned! Amazed, I watched as an opponent of the war was accorded adequate time to articulate and contextualize his responses, and a proponent was asked if not hardball follow-up questions, at least challenges lacking throughout the rest of television.

Journalist Morley Safer, of CBS' *60 Minutes,* calls Rose's program "the last refuge of intelligent conversation on television." Guests on the show include major international political figures and a mixture of renowned personalities from literature, theatre, film, dance, fashion, sports, science, medicine, and business—ranging from international statesmen Nelson Mandela and Mikhail Gorbachev to Nobel laureates Toni Morrison and Seamus Heaney to leaders in business like Bill Gates and Andy Grove.

Michael Apted

The best interviewer of all (since Socrates perhaps) is prolific English director/producer/writer Michael Apted. In his series of *Up* documentaries (*Seven Up, 7 Plus Seven, 21 Up, 28 Up, 35 Up* . . .), Apted has asked compassionate but diamond-cutting questions of the people he has tracked through their lives, visiting them every seven years since 1964, when they were seven-year-old kids. As of now, seven of his *Up* films have been made; Apted hopes to make an eighth (*56 Up*).

Born in 1941 in Aylesbury, England, Apted started his screen career working for Granada television, where he quickly climbed the ladder from researcher to director. His debut as a film director came in 1972. Since then, he has made numerous acclaimed documentaries and fictional features, more than a few of which deal with ethical and social concerns. Among his popular film directing credits are *Agatha, Coal Miner's Daughter, Gorky Park, Gorillas in the Mist, Incident at Oglala, Nell, Extreme Measures, The World Is Not Enough,* and *Amazing Grace.*

Appendix 2

Further Study

If you are compelled to go further in your study of the interview, again, I salute you! Here are some starting points for connecting to the global world of journalism and media. This is by no means an exhaustive list, but rather an indication of how many resources are available, of both information and good people.

International Center for Journalists
1616 H St. NW, Third Floor
Washington, DC 20006
http://www.icfj.org
The International Center for Journalists was founded in 1984 as an independent, nonprofit organization dedicated to improving the quality of journalism worldwide, especially in countries with little or no tradition of an independent press.

Journalism Education Association
Kansas State University, 103 Kedzie Hall
Manhattan, KS 66506-1505
http://www.jea.org
The Journalism Education Association is the only independent national scholastic journalism organization for teachers and advisers. The JEA supports free and responsible scholastic journalism by providing resources and educational opportunities, by promoting professionalism, by encouraging and rewarding student excellence and teacher achievement, and by fostering an atmosphere which encompasses diversity yet builds unity.

Society of Environmental Journalists
P.O. Box 2492
Jenkintown, PA 19046
http://www.sej.org
The Society of Environmental Journalists is the only U.S.-based member-ship organization of working journalists dedicated to improvements in environmental reporting. SEJ programs are designed to build a stronger, better-educated, and more closely connected network of professional jour-nalists and editors who cover the environment and environment-related issues. SEJ's primary goal is to advance public understanding of critically important environmental issues through more and better environmental journalism.

Project for Excellence in Journalism
1900 M St. NW, Suite 210
Washington, DC 20036
http://www.journalism.org
The Project for Excellence in Journalism was created in September 1996 to develop initiatives that would clarify ways journalists could better do their job.

The Poynter Institute
801 Third St. South
St. Petersburg, FL 33701
http://www.poynter.org
The Poynter Institute is a school dedicated to teaching and inspiring jour-nalists and media leaders. It promotes excellence and integrity in the practice of craft and in the practical leadership of successful businesses. It stands for a journalism that informs citizens and enlightens public discourse. It carries forward Nelson Poynter's belief in the value of inde-pendent journalism.

Society of Professional Journalists
Eugene S. Pulliam National Journalism Center
3909 N. Meridian St.
Indianapolis, IN 46208
http://www.spj.org

It is the mission of the Society of Professional Journalists:

- *To promote this flow of information.*
- *To maintain constant vigilance in protection of the First Amendment guarantees of freedom of speech and of the press.*
- *To stimulate high standards and ethical behavior in the practice of journalism.*
- *To foster excellence among journalists.*
- *To inspire successive generations of talented individuals to become dedicated journalists.*
- *To encourage diversity in journalism.*
- *To be the pre-eminent, broad-based membership organization for journalists.*
- *To encourage a climate in which journalism can be practiced freely.*

Index

About the Author

Martin Perlich has interviewed leaders in the fields of arts, entertainment, politics, and sports since 1965.

He was the first Intermission Host of the internationally syndicated *Cleveland Orchestra Broadcasts,* for which he interviewed myriad classical music luminaries. At radio stations in Cleveland and Los Angeles during the '60s and '70s, his interview subjects included such pivotal social and arts figures as Jane Fonda, Phil Ochs, members of the Black Panther Party, Attica prisoners, and Frank Zappa.

In 1975 he became Creative Consultant for NBC's hit show *The Midnight Special* (which he also wrote, rehearsed, and edited). At PBS's KCET-TV and WNET-TV, Perlich developed and produced dramatic, music, and documentary programming, including *Citizen Artist, Hollywood 90, Singer/Songwriter,* and *Informance.* As an independent film producer, he has developed projects for Lions Gate and his own company, including *The Trial of Ramona Africa,* starring Whoopi Goldberg, for Channel 4/London and American Playhouse. In the early '90s Perlich wrote, produced and directed interactive video for Warner New Media, including the CD-ROMs of Brahms' *A German Requiem,* Carl Orff's *Carmina Burana,* and the extensive educational project *The Orchestra.*

Currently, Perlich produces radio shows for the Los Angeles-area public radio station KCSN, where he is the Program Director. Among these shows is the award-winning series *Martin Perlich Interviews,* for which his guests have included Carl Sagan, Martin Scorsese, Marcel Ophüls, Whoopi Goldberg, Pierre Boulez, Terry Riley, John Adams, Joshua Bell, Placido Domingo, Bill Evans, Barry Gordy, Stevie Wonder, Tom Waits, Peter Townshend, Gore Vidal, and a vast array of other world-class creative people.

Perlich is also a competent amateur pianist and the author of the recently published novel *Wild Times.*